SECRET
LANDSCAPES

SECRET
LANDSCAPES

Mysterious Sites, Deserted Villages,
and Forgotten Places of
Great Britain and Ireland

WYNFORD VAUGHAN-THOMAS
and
MICHAEL HALES

SELECT
EDITIONS

This edition published 1992 by the Promotional Reprint Company
Limited, exclusively for Selecta Book Limited, Devizes, UK.

Copyright © Webb & Bower (Publishers) Limited 1980

ISBN 1 85648 080 1

Printed and Bound in Malaysia

HALF TITLE PAGE: **The Isle of Muck from the Isle of Eigg,
Inner Hebrides**

TITLE PAGE: **Clifden Castle, County Galway**

THIS PAGE: **The remaining columns of the peat store, Old
Gang Smelt Mill, Swaledale, Yorkshire**

CONTENTS

Rusland wood, once the site of charcoal burning

INTRODUCTION

Grey recumbent tombs of the dead in desert places
Standing stones on the vacant wine-red moor,
Hills of sheep, and the homes of the silent vanished races
And winds, austere, and pure . . .

Those cleansing winds of Robert Louis Stevenson's poem still flow over the secret landscapes of the islands of Britain. They stir the heather around the grey cromlechs scattered over the dark Presely Hills of West Wales. They whistle around the lichen-covered walls of ruined abbeys on remote headlands of Ireland's Atlantic coast, or set the rusting wires moaning in abandoned lead mines high up in the valleys of the Northern Pennines. In these long-forgotten, lonely places our ancestors lived, worked, fought, worshipped and died. All that remains, in many of the sites, are a few tumbled stones or a broken wall and a shattered cross. The folk who passed their lives here may have left no recorded history, yet these cromlechs, ruined towers and walls are as much a part of our national heritage as are the great cathedrals or the eighteenth-century elegance of Bath. Their mysterious charm is increased by the loneliness of their setting. You have to, as it were, go on pilgrimage to appreciate them.

We are lucky to live in an ancient land. Over vast areas of the earth's surface you feel that man is a comparative newcomer. As you travel across the endless prairies of America's Middle West, no structure that you see, no artificial mark on the face of the land, can be more than a hundred and fifty years old. Our islands are strikingly different. Here the landscape is a palimpsest – a parchment used again and again by the long procession of races that moved across these islands for thousands of years of our history. They have all left traces of their presence, sometimes clearly superimposed, sometimes with the early remains almost obliterated by later occupation of the same site. In recent

7

years, archaeologists have made spectacular advances in the readings of the various layers of the palimpsest. They show us the early hunters arriving again as the glaciers of the last Ice Age retreated to the lost fastnesses of the mountains of Western Britain. Then the harbingers of the Neolithic agricultural revolution ventured across the newly-opened English Channel in their frail skin boats. Onward through thousands of years, successive waves of newcomers came to take possession of the land, to mix with the people already there or to drive them further westwards until the Atlantic coastline halted all further progress. In this long march across our landscape, the Celts and the Anglo-Saxons are very late arrivals indeed. We have to wait later still before we get the first reliable written records of the people who fashioned the landscape of Britain.

Somehow or other, it is not always the well-documented sites that set the imagination racing; it is often on the smaller, remoter sites, where few people come, that the past seems to merge with the present and our ancestors seem very near. Inevitably, the more famous and accessible sites like Stonehenge or Avebury are under pressure. More than 800,000 people visited Stonehenge in 1979, and the Department of the Environment has had no option but to surround it with a high fence and build a car park with a tunnel under the main road. The noblest stone circle in Europe has lost the original glory of its setting in the wide bareness of Salisbury Plain. You have to work hard to recapture the awe and delight with which the early pioneers of archaeology examined it at the end of the seventeenth century. That most sympathetic, if somewhat charmingly woolly-minded chronicler, John Aubrey, was the first to measure it seriously. He wrote with moving modesty: 'This inquiry, I must confess is a groping in the dark; but although I have not brought it into a clear light: yet I can affirm that I have brought it from an utter darkness to a thin mist.' It was William Stukeley who started that long association between Stonehenge and the Druids that was to be-devil the early

ABOVE: *Carnasserie Castle, Strathclyde, view from the south*

8

science of archaeology for two hundred years.

The mist gets thinner with every year that passes. The modern archaeologist, armed with new techniques of excavation and radiocarbon dating, can reply to our questions about these 'reliques of things past' with a certainty to which Aubrey, Stukeley and the other early inquirers could lay no pretensions. But this new certainty cannot destroy the mystery and fascination of lost stones in lonely places. It is not only the cromlechs, the barrows and the other precious prehistoric remains that help to create the secret landscapes of Britain; later builders have left evidence of their presence in hill forts, castle towers, ruined churches and in the wreckage of old lead mines in lonely recesses of the high hills. Even in our own day the firing ranges used by the army are creating their own secret landscapes, where time has had to stand still under gunfire, and future generations may well turn to them to see what our land looked like as the twentieth century ended.

Michael Hales is an artist with the camera, who has a gift for capturing the moods of the British and Irish countryside. He has long been fascinated by the relics of the past in lonely places. His pictures portray them, not only in the bright clear sun of summer, but in all phases of our changeable weather. The great standing stones of the Ring of Brodgar, in the treeless landscape of the Orkneys, gather weight and power when set under darkening skies. He has deliberately sought out some of the more remote and unfamiliar sites where the rare visitor can feel again for himself the authentic thrill of discovery and speculation, and can perhaps chuckle with old John Aubrey when he wrote, 'It is strange that so eminent an antiquitie should be so long unguarded by our chorographers'.

As he searched for the unfamiliar, Michael Hales went naturally to the wilder parts of the islands of Britain, especially to the Celtic west of Scotland and Ireland. He has also included some not so well known antiquities in England and Wales. Through his skill

TOP: *Lonely landscape near Loch Michean, Strathclyde*

9

The remains of the Devon fishing village of Hallsands

with the camera, it seems, he makes us see everything with a new understanding.

The photographs fall naturally into six sections. The first section, Living Places, covers the places where man has lived through the long centuries and then, from a variety of causes, eventually abandoned the struggle. The deserted crofts of Skye and the ruined tower of the 'broch' of Dun Carloway in the Outer Hebrides find their place naturally beside the abandoned village of Hallsands in South Devon, threatened by the sea in our own time. The second section, Fortifications, reflects the way man has striven to defend himself in an unfriendly world. Again Michael Hales has sought the earlier and unfamiliar examples – the Iron Age forts perched on the summits of wild crags on the west coast of Scotland, the

lonely towers along the shores of the Shannon estuary, or the great circular forts of the Gaeltach in Ireland – those strange masterpieces of the art of dry stone walling. The places where man has worked – sometimes profitably, sometimes with his dream of El Dorado bitterly disappointed – can be as romantic as the castles and the burial chambers. There is no need to go to the remote prehistoric past to find the picturesque ruins of industry. The nineteenth century can supply them in plenty, from the abandoned coke ovens of the early days of the Industrial Revolution to the deserted lead mines, with their great wheels rusting and ivy growing over the once busy crushing plants.

After work comes worship. From the very first moment that they settled in these islands, the primitive farmers must have tried to solve the eternal puzzle of our life on Earth. The solutions to the mystery have

changed as the centuries pass by, but any form of worship, however primitive, involves ritual. As the rituals became more complicated, they demanded a place in which they could be celebrated. The great stone circles and the lone standing stones, scattered over the western moorlands of Britain must surely have had some religious significance. What other force would have moved men to drag the huge trilithons of Stonehenge into position across miles of country, or have inspired them to set up the great stones of Callanish? Recently Professor Alexander Thom has made accurate measurements of many of our stone circles and given new life to the theory that they may have had some astronomical purpose. The experts are still arguing; the visitor can only marvel at them and feel their mysterious power.

When we come to the early Christian monuments of Britain – from ruined abbeys to broken crosses – we feel that we are on firmer ground. At least we know the faith that inspired the men who constructed them. Our hearts go out to those early Irish monks in their beehive cells on the savage crag of Skellig Michael, in the midst of the lonely waters of Ireland's Atlantic coast. We can still worship where St Columba knelt on the holy island of Iona in Scotland. We can sympathize with the motives that led the good abbot of Corcomroe to build the delicate Irish Romanesque vaulting in the choir of his great church, set in the stern, limestone landscape of County Clare.

But pagan or Christian, in the end we must lie down when our time comes and, willingly or unwillingly, take our rest. The early graveyards and the great prehistoric barrows are never unhappy places. Here lie our remote ancestors and, as we walk through the low graves and the weathered mediaeval crosses, they seem to speak directly to us. As indeed do all the tumbled stones, broken walls and noble cromlechs that are illustrated in this book.

Secret Landscapes is thus, not a guide book to the archaeological sites of Britain. A large number of excellent guides, written by experts, are readily available, and we have included a short selection of them as an appendix, together with a glossary of the simpler archaeological terms. Photographing sites so as to catch the spirit of the place is not easy. It is still more difficult to get a new angle on some of the familiar archaeological showplaces of Britain. One particular section of Hadrian's Wall seems to have climbed over Hotbank Crags, near Housesteads, to please photographers since the first portable cameras were developed. Michael Hales has therefore added some helpful technical notes on his own experiences while trying to penetrate the atmosphere of our less familiar treasures in stone. That is, after all, the theme of this book. The best way to capture the true spirit of our past is to turn away from the well worn tracks and explore the secret landscapes of Britain for oneself.

LIVING PLACES

The hall of Cynddylan is dark tonight
Without fire, without bed;
I shall weep a while and then be silent.
NINTH CENTURY WELSH EPIC POEM

DUN CARLOWAY, ISLE OF LEWIS, OUTER
HEBRIDES

CLOCHÁN NA CARRAIGE, INISHMORE, ARAN
ISLANDS

A CHEVIOT HILL ENCLOSURE,
NORTHUMBERLAND

LULWORTH, DORSET

THE LONE SHIELING, EIGG, INNER HEBRIDES

DIN LLIGWY, ANGLESEY, GWYNEDD

HALLSANDS, DEVON

THE RUINED BLACK HOUSE, SKYE

GLEN GLOY, ISLE OF ARRAN

DUN NAN GALL BROCH, ISLE OF MULL

BRAY TOWER, VALENCIA ISLAND

The sun bursts through the cloud above the Isle of Muck, Inner Hebrides

A section of Dun Carloway's double wall

Dun carloway broch, isle of lewis, outer hebrides. The broch was a circular fortified dwelling peculiar to Scotland and mainly found in the north-western part of the country and on the Outer Isles. The outer wall has, as it were, a double skin and was constructed on the dry-stone principle. The structure may have been first devised by that mysterious race, the Picts. Most brochs seem to date from the period when Scotland was being slowly converted to Christianity, although some of them may well be pre-Christian. Inside their curious circular tower the broch-dwellers – in the words of Richard Feachem – must have felt 'like the tender meat of a crustacean secure within the hard shell'.

The Dun Carloway example is one of the

A general view of the dun

best preserved of the Scottish brochs, and although the stones were plundered in the past, part of the outer wall still stands about thirty feet above the ground. The characteristic double walls are clearly seen, as are the entrance passage and the interior staircase. Dr Euan Mackie, the authority on brochs, pointed out that apart from Stonehenge, the broch is 'the only really advanced architec-tural creation of prehistoric and early historic times which was invented entirely within Britain . . . it is Man's greatest architectural achievement in dry stone masonry'.

Looking from Dun Carloway across the lonely landscape which surrounds it

CLOCHÁN NA CARRAIGE, INISHMORE, ARAN ISLANDS. This beehive hut stands in the midst of a complex pattern of limestone walls on Inishmore, the largest of the three Aran Islands that stand 'like a breakwater at the entrance of Galway Bay'. It is one of the best surviving examples of a form of dwelling which was once common on the islands and may date back to the old monks' cells so characteristic of early monasticism.

In many of the fields around Clochán na Carraige the earth was literally 'made' by the islanders. Seaweed and sand were carted up in creels on donkeys or on human backs and the sparse soil was scraped out from the cracks in the rocks and carefully spread upon the lower layer. In such a stony landscape, there was no possibility of using timber for housing.

Writing in 1684, Roderick O'Flaherty, to whom we owe the first description of the Arans, gives a charming account of the way of life of the old Aran Islanders. 'They have cloghans, a kind of building of stones laid one upon the other which are brought to a roof without any manner of mortar to cement them, some of which cabins will hold forty men on their floor; so ancient that nobody knows how long ago any of them was made. Scarcity of wood and store of fit stones, without peradventure found out the first invention.'

ABOVE: *A beehive hut at Clochán na Carraige*
LEFT: *The fields surrounding Clochán na Carraige*

A CHEVIOT HILL ENCLOSURE, NORTHUMBERLAND. This strange enclosure lies high up on the wild moorlands of the Cheviot Hills close to the actual border between England and Scotland. A small Iron Age settlement? A border stronghold? Who can be certain? A few miles away the hills roll to their highest point, the Cheviot itself, at 2676 ft. The wind moans through the gnarled trees of the small plantation which alone breaks the flowing lines of this high grassy wilderness. The sturdy, short-legged Cheviot sheep are now the only inhabitants, but whoever dwelt or worked here in the old days would have known to the full all the romance of the uncertain border life as revealed in the old ballads.

Did Earl Douglas march this way to his fateful meeting with the Earl of Northumberland in the wild hunting of Chevy Chase?

> Of fifteen hundred Englishmen
> Went home but fifty-three,
> The rest in Chevy Chase were slain
> Under the green-woode tree.

Not so many miles to the east of this spot the river Till rises and curves around the foot of the Cheviot to meet the bigger Tweed. It flows past the tragic field of Flodden, where the English took full and shattering revenge on the Scots.

> Said Tweed to Till, 'Why rin ye so still?'
> Said Till to Tweed, 'Though ye rin with
>   speed
> And I rin slaw
> For aye man that ye droon,
> I droon twa.'

The rhythm of the old ballads seems to accompany your steps past this enclosure and on to the lonely heights of the Cheviot.

ABOVE: *View of the enclosure, which lies just behind the dry stone wall, from a nearby wood*

LEFT: *The remaining walls of the enclosure seen from across the valley*

ABOVE: *The boarded-up houses of Tyneham Village*
ABOVE RIGHT: *The Rectory, Tyneham village*

LULWORTH, DORSET. Not all abandoned settlements date back to Neolithic or even mediaeval times. Our own age has also added its quota; and prominent among the ruin-makers is the Army. It is not the Army's fault; it has to find somewhere to fire its guns and inevitably it is compelled to take over some delectable piece of the land. Some conservationists even look on the bright side of the military takeover. I remember walking with a keen country lover on the edge of the vast firing range that has taken over the Epynt in Mid-Wales. As the guns thundered in the distance, he declared, 'Well, better the Army than the forestry. The guns will go away one day, but these endless miles of bloody giant matchsticks

are here for ever.' True enough. Even where
the Army still operates, the villages isolated
in the ranges still seem to be ready to return
to civilian life if given half a chance. Imber
on Salisbury Plain is a case in point; Lulworth on the Dorset coast is another.

Lulworth has long been regarded as one of
the showplace beauty spots on the South
Coast. The cove is a remarkable geological
freak. The sea has, by cutting a narrow passage through the hard Purbeck limestone,
reached and hollowed out a large bowl in the
softer chalk behind. The tourists still flock to
see it, but part of the area, including the village, is in the hands of the Army. Some
houses have suffered severely from neglect,
others look as if the owner would step out at

any moment to ask you in for a cup of tea.
Services are still held in the church on special
occasions. Everything seems to await the
time when Lulworth will abandon its role as
a secret landscape and go public again.

Anti-tank defences on the sea shore near Lulworth

THE LONE SHIELING, EIGG, INNER HEBRIDES. Eigg is the small but beautiful island lying south of Skye, in company with those other curiously named islands so beloved by schoolboys in geography lessons, Rum and Muck. The abandoned crofting settlement of the Gruliuns lies on the high ground looking out over the sea towards Muck. The remains of the buildings and the walls that once formed the pens for the highland cattle now lie among the tumbled rocks. It is a place of rare beauty yet of infinite sadness.

Eigg, in common with so many places in the West of Scotland, suffered from the notorious Highland Clearances. From about 1760 onwards, the landlords found that sheep were more profitable than men. The old clan system, following the failure of the 1745 rising, had been broken for ever and the clan chiefs now had no need for the loyalty of scores of poor but proud crofters.

All through the late eighteenth and early nineteenth centuries the Clearances gathered momentum, culminating in the notorious Sutherland Clearances in the first part of the reign of Queen Victoria. Ironically, the sheep themselves were 'cleared' from some parts of the Highlands, after Prince Albert's example and Sir Edwin Landseer's painting had made 'deer stalking' fashionable.

The Clearance on Eigg came later and was not so violent but was none the less effective. The Macdonald family's lease terminated and fifteen small crofting settlements, including the Gruliuns, were cleared to make room for one sheep farm, let to a lowland farmer, Stephen Stewart. Old inhabitants still tell you how their fathers remembered Stewart's boasting that 'so sweet were the grasses that grew there that all his ewes had twins'. The displaced men sought new pastures in Canada and elsewhere.

As you walk among the low broken walls, the words of the 'Canadian Boat Song' no longer seem hackneyed.

From the lone shieling of the misty island,
Mountains divide us, and the waste of seas –
Yet still the blood is strong, the heart is
   Highland,
And we in dreams behold the Hebrides.

ABOVE: *An Sgurr forms an imposing backdrop to the remains
of crofts deserted during the Highland Clearances*
OVERLEAF: *The remains of dry stone walls built to enclose
sheep in the Gruluins*

27

IN LLIGWY, ANGLESEY, GWYNEDD. A series of huts surrounded by a wall set in woodlands on a rocky ridge in the island of Anglesey, Din Lligwy may have been the residence of a native chief who was a client of Rome. The Roman power was maintained in North Wales from the powerful fortress of Segontium at the north-western end of the Menai Straits. The chieftain at Din Lligwy may have made his money by smelting iron for the Romans, since the remains of a forge have been found in one of the huts.

But by the fourth century the imperial power of Rome began to wane. Our petty chief of Din Lligwy began to feel unsafe as the wild Irish started to raid the Anglesey coast. He surrounded his headquarters with a strong wall and hoped for the best. Alas, we know that the Romans withdrew from Segontium at around AD 385. Did the chieftain of Din Lligwy succeed in holding out against the Irish? Later, describing the Irish attackers, the monk Gildas said 'their hulls might be seen creeping across the glassy surface of the main like so many insects awakened from torpor by the heat of the noonday sun and making with one accord for some familiar haunt'. Did the invaders finally overwhelm Din Lligwy with fire and slaughter? The quiet stones among the trees can give us no answer.

The remains of Din Lligwy

HALLSANDS, DEVON. Secret landscapes can be created dramatically in our own time. A national catastrophe can reduce a settlement to ruin. Within twenty years ivy starts to cover the abandoned walls with soothing green, the grass appears through the cracked hearthstones and trees surround the once busy village. Within fifty years the site will be taking its place with Anglo-Saxon hamlets and Welsh drystone huts as one of the lost villages of Britain. This was the fate of Hallsands, a once busy fishing village on the South Devon coast.

Hallsands was built under the cliffs and was protected from the sea by an extensive shingle bank. The inhabitants were fishermen who, when the shoals came inshore during the season, caught herring in seine nets but throughout the rest of the year relied on crabbing.

The village lived simply and happily on its fishing until 1898, when a licence was granted allowing shingle, needed for use in building the extension to the dockyard at Devonport, to be taken from the bank protecting Hallsands. The villagers were assured that the sea would replace the shingle from the local rocks, but the Board of Trade's research had been inadequate. The shingle, deposited in the bay, was brought there in prehistoric times and cannot be replaced. The dredger eventually removed 650,000 tons of shingle, with the inevitable result. In 1901 part of the sea-wall was undermined. The furious fishermen cast off the mooring ropes that anchored the dredger to the shore and the contractors had to give up the work. Too late, the damage was done. With the protection of its shingle bank gone, Hallsands awaited its end. Successive storms breached the sea-wall. In 1904 the southern end of Hallsands could only be reached by a wooden bridge. In 1917 came final disaster. A great storm hit the coast; as the water crashed through the inadequate defences, the fishermen escaped to higher ground and next morning saw the last of their thirty houses crumble into the tide.

THE RUINED BLACK HOUSE, SKYE. Skye's mountain scenery has earned it the reputation of being the wildest of the Hebridean islands. The Cuillin ridge is unrivalled in Britain for the savage grandeur of its rock scenery. To see the mist curling among the jagged 3000 ft peaks of the Cuillin from the shore of Loch Coruisk is a rare mountaineering experience. At the point where the tumbling waters of Glen Sligachan turn into Harta Corrie, a track climbs over the col that leads down to Loch Creitheach. Here lie the ruins of this ancient shieling, with the sharp summit of Sgurr nan Gillean in the distant background. Once it was an inhabited, busy settlement although hardly prosperous. Life on Skye, by lowland standards, was always hard, if often happy. The redoubtable Doctor Johnson came to Skye with his companion Boswell, and they saw something of the life of the Highlanders through the curtain of rain that accompanied most of their visit. Boswell described a typical Skye house:

> The walls of the cottages in Sky [so Boswell spells it] instead of being one compacted mass of stones, are often formed by two exterior surfaces of stone, filled up with earth in the middle, which makes them very warm. The roof is generally bad. They are thatched, sometimes with straw sometimes with heath, sometimes with fern. The thatch is secured by ropes of straw, or of heath; and to fix the ropes, there is a stone tied to the end of each. These stones hang around the bottom of the roof, and make it look like a lady's hair in papers.

Later in their tour, Boswell and Johnson went into a 'black house' on the island of Coll. 'There was but one bed for the family and the hut was very smoky.' The Doctor was naturally ready with a classical quotation: *Et hoc secundum sententiam philosophorum est esse beatus.* (This according to the ideas of the philosophers is to be happy.) Said Boswell, 'The philosophers, when they placed happiness in a cottage, supposed cleanliness and no smoke.' Johnson replied, 'Sir, they did not think about either.'

The sharp summit of Sgurr nan Gillean

ABOVE: *A grass-covered makeshift house in front of an old dry stone pen*

RIGHT: *The sun breaks through over Glen Gloy, near the homestead shown above*

G LEN GLOY, ISLE OF ARRAN. Arran is the superb island that dominates the wide Firth of Clyde. 'Arran of the many stags' the Gaelic poets called it; the early seventeenth-century writer who rejoiced in the strange name of Lugless Willie Lithgow wrote this panegyric on the view from the high summits:

> This island is sur-clouded with Goatfellhill which with wide eyes overlooked the western continent and the northern country of Ireland; bringing also into sight on a clear summer's day, the Isle of Man and the higher coast of Cumberland. A larger prospect no mountain in the world can show, pointing out three Kingdoms at one sight; neither is there any isle like to it for brave gentry, good archers and hill-hovering hunters.

After Lugless Willie's praise, it is no wonder that Arran has become a popular holiday island.

But islands have an irresistible attraction to others besides those in search of a short holiday. Arran has seemed to many people the right place in which to rebuild their lives – to start again and simplify the whole complicated business of earning a living. Some twelve years ago a young couple decided to 'get out of the rat race'. After finding a deserted spot at the top of Glen Gloy, the couple, expecting no luxury, set out to live the 'simple life'. They struggled to make a little money by making furniture; a struggle that proved to be too difficult. The 'simple lifers' were driven back to the city. The homestead in Glen Gloy with its view over the high hills and down to the sea is still there; a quiet witness to the real difficulties of 'escape'.

Across Loch Tuath towards the Isle of Ulva

DUN NAN GALL BROCH, ISLE OF MULL. Not all the old Pictish brochs of the northwest of Scotland are as well preserved as Dun Carloway on Lewis or the impressive broch of Mousa in the Shetlands. There are, after all, between five and six hundred sites recorded, many of which have not yet been carefully studied or surveyed. Dun nan Gall Broch, on the Island of Mull, is certainly more ruined than Dun Carloway, but the double wall, so characteristic of the broch construction, is easily traced. A bar-hole is visible at the entrance, showing the primitive method that was used to hold the door in position.

The site is impressive. Dun nan Gall stands on a rocky headland above the dark waters of Loch Tuath and beyond lies the island of Ulva, whose chieftain – in the once famous poem by Thomas Campbell – eloped with Lord Ullin's daughter with pre-

This pile of rubble is all that remains of the broch of Dun nan Gall

dictably unfortunate results. Mull itself is the second largest of the Inner Hebrides and the coastline is so indented that it measures 250 miles in circumference.

The Picts, who created the brochs, were pushed out of Mull and eventually out of a big area of Western Scotland during the sixth century AD. The newcomers, the Scotti from Northern Ireland, eventually gave their name to the whole country and imposed on the Western Isles their own form of Gaelic. The eighth century saw the beginning of the Viking raids and it was not until comparatively late that the King of Scotland became the Lord of the Isles. Thus, the old broch of Dun nan Gall has seen much history pass its ruined walls.

B RAY TOWER, VALENCIA ISLAND. Valencia
Island lies off the Inveragh peninsula in
western Kerry. The curious name has no
Spanish connections. It is an anglicized form
of the old Gaelic *Bheil Inse* – 'the island at the
mouth of the river'. Valencia is joined to the
mainland by a bridge and has developed its
tourist industry. However, it still remains a
quiet, withdrawn place with an astonishing-
ly mild climate in winter. It only attracted
the attention of the outside world in 1858,
when it became the starting point of the first
transatlantic cable to Newfoundland. The
little settlement of Knightstown was
selected as the eastern terminal because the
harbour is the most westerly one in Europe.

The island has a varied coastline and the
flower-covered moorlands in the north rise
to 888 ft, giving magnificent views over the
mountains of Kerry. The western end of
Valencia is equally impressive: Bray Head
plunges into the Atlantic and on its summit
is an abandoned look-out tower, probably
built during the period of English control.
As you stand by the dark walls and listen to
the sound of the ever restless sea, you feel
that you have reached the very edge of old
historic Europe. As the mists close around,
you share the feeling of awe that possessed
the first Celtic newcomers who may have
stood here over 2000 years ago. Beyond lies
mystery; the unknown world.

FORTIFICATIONS

For old, unhappy, far-off things
And battles long ago.
WILLIAM WORDSWORTH

The central fortifications of Dun Aengus, Inishmore

DUN AENGUS FORT, ARAN ISLANDS. It is one of the ironies of history that as soon as man gave up hunting and settled down to agriculture, he felt the need to defend himself. First with primitive palisades, then with earthworks and then with walls and towers. The attack of the sword demanded the defence of the stone and nowhere can you see a more remarkable defence than at the fort of Dun Aengus on Inishmore in the Aran Islands.

The setting is breathtaking. The fort consists of three concentric semi-circles of massive drystone walling set on the very edge of a 200 ft high sea cliff. The cliff is so steep that the Aran Islanders drop their fishing lines from the top of it straight into the sea. It has been said that the semi-circular shape of Dun Aengus is the result of a cliff-fall which cut through the original circular fort like a knife. However, it seems more likely that the semi-circular form was deliberately chosen and that the ends of the walls were carefully anchored onto that fearful cliff-drop. The wall of the inner keep is 18 ft high and 13 ft thick. Between the second and third wall is what the old mediaeval castle-builders would have called a *chevaux de frise* – a series of limestone slabs set on edge which would make it very difficult for an attacker to approach the wall or drive away cattle after he had broken in. The modern visitor will be immediately reminded of the anti-tank 'dragons' teeth' of the Maginot Line.

Who was the Aengus after whom the fort was named? The old writers maintained that he was the leader of the Fir Bolg, the race that held Ireland – according to legend – before the final Laganian invasion around the third century BC. Here Aengus and the Fir Bolg made their last stand since 'nothing but massacre, or drowning in the Atlantic deeps, awaited them outside their island fortress'. Modern archaeologists have discounted this romantic story. Dun Aengus is nothing more than a magnificent example of the typical Irish ring fort which was an indigenous invention of late Neolithic times but which continued to be constructed as late as the seventeenth century. Here a petty chief-

tain could live, and drive in his cattle and shelter his followers in the event of a piratical raid. No matter, Dun Aengus is magnificent, even if we don't know when, or by whom it was built.

The three outer defences of Dun Aengus

46

47

RIGHT: The last remains of the
fortifications on An Sgurr

ABOVE: *The bleak landscape of the Isle of Eigg towards the Isle of Rhum*

An Sgurr Hill Fort, Eigg, Inner Hebrides. Forts and castles all seem to be sited with a cunning eye for dramatic impact or scenic splendour. We remember Stirling Castle perched on its defiant rock facing the wild Highlands and the Roman Wall, writhing its way like a stone snake over the moorlands of Northumberland. Of course, the old builders were influenced by no romantic considerations. They were simply looking for the best defensive positions, and, in the mountainous west of Britain,

convenience and romance coincide. No hill fort has a more magnificent site than the tumbled walls that crown An Sgurr, on the small island of Eigg in the Inner Hebrides.

An Sgurr is the extraordinary hill, rising to 1289 ft, that dominates the island and forms one of the most remarkable geological formations in Scotland. It is an enormous tower of columnar pitchstone porphyry, almost undercut at its base with cliffs that drop 400 ft from the summit. On the lower slopes to the west lies a strange cluster of small lakes among the rocks. The Gaelic speakers tell of the dangerous and mysterious fairy horses that can emerge from their depths.

After all this, the actual fortifications are slightly unimpressive; just a line of heaped stones, the remains of a 10 ft thick wall which ran between the northern and southern precipices of the Sgurr. Perhaps the very term 'fort' is misleading. It conjures up pictures of strong walls and towers laid out by a skilled military architect. These early hill 'forts' were more primitive affairs. They were built as a refuge in time of danger; a place where the women, children and the cattle could be safely collected. Permanent residence on top of the Sgurr would hardly be attractive, even in tough Iron Age days.

But the tradition of taking refuge when danger threatened continued for a long time on Eigg. In 1577, so the story goes, all the 396 inhabitants took refuge in a cave below the Sgurr from a revengeful party of Macleods. The Macleods after detecting their presence by a track in the snow, lit a fire at the mouth of the cave and suffocated them all. Ever since, the cave has been known as the Cave of Tears.

The Massacre of Eigg has passed into Highland tradition, but as usual, the historians have raised a whole series of tricky points about it. As you stand on the summit of the Sgurr and look down towards the Cave of Tears it is easy to sympathize with the comment made by the Free Church Minister of Eigg: 'the less I inquire into its history . . . the more I was likely to feel I know something about it.'

49

CHEW GREEN ROMAN CAMP, NORTHUMBER-LAND. A small Roman camp high up on the Cheviots near the Scottish border. Detachments of the legions would have halted briefly here on their way to join their units stationed on the Antonine Wall a hundred miles to the north. Probably the first Romans to tramp over these bleak moorlands were the men of the army led by the great commander Julius Agricola. We know a great deal about him because he was lucky enough to have the historian Tacitus as his son-in-law. Agricola led his men on over the Cheviots and, after tough campaigning, smashed the native forces in the battle of Mons Graupius. Agricola won the victory

and Tacitus coined the epigram: 'They make a desert and call it peace.'

The Antonine Wall was built about fifty years later towards the end of the 130s AD across that narrow neck of Scotland between the Firths of Forth and Clyde. It proved to be too ambitious; in AD 158 the Scottish wall was abandoned and the Romans fell back to their first defensive line. They made punitive expeditions northward from time to time, but the legions had ceased to worry about this small stopping place lost on the moors. Late in the fourth century the Empire's defences broke. It was then the turn of Rome to become a desert with no peace.

CAHERCOMMAUN STONE FORT, COUNTY CLARE. This is a slightly smaller edition of the Dun Aengus fort on the Aran Islands. Cahercommaun is built on the cliff edge of a steep valley in the barren limestone region of the Burren in County Clare. Like Dun Aengus it consists of three walls; the two outermost being semi-circles and anchored to the cliff-edge. The innermost wall, unlike the central fortification of Dun Aengus, forms an almost complete circle. When the fort was excavated in 1934 the remains of a series of beehive huts were found. This reinforced the theory that many of these ring structures were not necessarily built for military purposes, as were the later castles of

the Middle Ages, but as homesteads sheltered by a wall. The bigger forts would probably house a petty chieftain although, as with the smaller structures, the fortified walls only protected the usual farm buildings inside. Two of the huts had 'souterrains' – stone underground passages used for storage or as living quarters in some cases.

Cahercommaun is one of the largest of the hundreds of stone forts scattered over the rocky Burren area. As usual in the Burren, the way to it is not easy and could even be dangerous for someone not used to walking over rough country. Beware, there are rocks hidden under hazel bushes and no sign posts!

DUNADD, STRATHCLYDE. Dunadd stands on an isolated rocky hill that rises above the meadows of the river Add, a few miles north-west of Lochgilphead in Argyll. The remains consist of a series of walls set at different levels among the rocks. They are perhaps no more impressive than the ruins of many other duns scattered over the west and north-west of Scotland. However, Dunadd is one of the few examples of this kind of fortification that is actually mentioned in recorded history. The Irish *Annals*

of Ulster relates that in AD 683 a mixed force of Picts and Scots besieged a party of Britons here. Dunadd is also notable as the capital of the Kingdom of Dalriada, founded by the Scotti – the Irish tribe who invaded this part of mainland Scotland in the sixth century.

The King of Dalriada, Kenneth MacAlpine succeeded to the Pictish inheritance and gave the whole country the name of Scotland.

The Picts however, left their mark on Dunadd. Near the entrance of the inner defence line, symbols have been carved in the

ABOVE: *The rocky promontory of Dunadd rises out of the marshy plain*

rocks. One of them, a boar, is certainly of Pictish origin in a style dated to the late seventh and early eighth centuries. Were they incised as a symbol of victory after the siege of AD 683? There are other strange carvings including one of a human foot. No one has yet convincingly interpreted them; they add to the mystery of Dunadd.

T RE'R CEIRI, GWYNEDD. Tre'r Ceiri (the town of the giants), is a remarkable collection of stone huts perched on the southwest summit of Yŕ Eifl (1849 ft), a Welsh name wrongly translated into 'The Rivals'. These graceful triple peaks do, however, look as if they were battling for preeminence amongst the other peaks that range away from them in a long, ever lowering line down the Lleyn peninsula to the sea. The Iron Age settlement lies well above

the 1000 ft mark, and there is a steep climb up to it. The climb is most enjoyable in late summer when the rocky hillside is rich in tempting bilberries.

You pass through a series of ramparts to reach the top enclosure which contains a surprising number of small stone-walled huts. Although Tre'r Ceiri began as an Iron Age settlement surrounded by defences like a hill fort, a curious change occurred after the Romans conquered the area: many of the circular huts were enlarged, their shape altered to become almost rectangular and their number increased to a total of about a hundred and fifty. Were the Britons unconsciously imitating their new masters and exchanging their natural curves for the fashionable Roman straight lines?

RIGHT: *The remains of the entrance to the village of Tre'r Ceiri*
OVERLEAF: *The small huts and the surrounding walls of Tre'r Ceiri*

DUN ONAGHT, INISHMORE, ARAN ISLANDS. Again a typical Irish 'ring fort', rising impressively from among a maze of limestone walls on the longest of the Aran Islands. It has been restored but retains its air of belonging to the heyday of the old Celtic power in Ireland. These structures are almost impossible to date accurately. They could have been built as late as the sixteenth century or they could date back to the early days of the Celtic conquest of Ireland. The form remained unchanged because it suited the needs of a turbulent country. The farmer had to protect his livestock against wolf packs and himself against sudden raids from unfriendly neighbours. He enclosed his farm buildings with these solid walls and lived safely inside them. The very act of collecting the stones to build the forts made the fields around them more fertile.

These circular structures are very Celtic in spirit, and reflect in themselves one important fact about the history of Ireland: the Romans never conquered it or submitted it to their stern discipline.

The Romans naturally considered adding Ireland to their Empire. Agricola, who became governor of Roman Britain in AD 78, thought that the conquest would be easy. He already knew a great deal about the geography of the country, for Ptolemy's map, dating back to the second century BC, gives a good general idea of the island. He had also sent his fleet around northern Scotland and his sailors had passed close to the shores of Ireland. With this knowledge, and the fact that he had an exiled Irish prince in his camp – a convenient excuse for interfering in Irish politics – he sent an enthusiastic report to Rome. 'Give me one legion and I can quickly finish the job.' Not for the first time did a general give an over-optimistic estimate to his government. The Emperor, Vespasian, turned down his request. Although Tacitus, Agricola's son-in-law and admirer, hinted that this decision was influenced by jealousy of Agricola's achievements, the decision was probably a wise one. The Empire's military resources were becoming overstretched. It was time to consolidate existing frontiers.

ABOVE: *The rugged landscape around Dun Onaght*

The terraced walls of Dun Onaght

T RUSTY'S HILL FORT, DUMFRIES & GALLO-
WAY. Trusty's Hill is a small fort in the
south-west corner of Scotland not far from
the Solway Firth. The walls are vitrified and
the wooden buildings which once filled the
interior must have been burnt. The area is
roughly rectangular: 90 ft by 60 ft. The
south-east entrance lies between two natural
outcrops of rock on which Pictish symbols
have been carved. Although this area be-
longed to the Strathclyde power, whose

princes were Brythonic speaking, the Picts
also played an important part in the region.
The Picts were, after all, of Celtic stock
although the main base of their power lay in
the north and east of Scotland.

In this region, and at points in the south-
west like Trusty's Hill they have left a fascinating collection of inscribed stones behind
them. Pictish symbols include crescents,
horseshoes and triple-discs and also ser-
pents, wild boars and bulls, all depicted with

ABOVE: *The hillock, behind the sheep, is the site of Trusty's hill fort*
RIGHT: *These Pictish symbols are among those inscribed on the rocks at Trusty's hill fort*

stylized grace. Other shapes are derived from Christian manuscripts. No one has penetrated the mystery of their meaning. The Picts were crushingly defeated by the Norsemen in AD 839. They disappeared from history, taking with them the secrets of their inscribed stones.

CARROCK FELL HILL FORT, CUMBRIA. A late Iron Age fort placed in lonely country, on the northern edge of the Lake District. Behind it lies the 3000 ft range of Skiddaw and the shapely ridge of Blencathra or Saddleback. Sharp Edge, beloved of hill-walkers, leaps towards the summit like a knife-thrust. This is wild country and it is unlikely that a large population would have been attracted to a life on these bleak fells. The tribesmen probably used it as a refuge in time of trouble. The area protected by the wall was about five acres; enough to hold the cattle which could be driven up to it in the event of attack by raiders. The site was a good defensive one and may have even been used in the Bronze Age. How long did it continue to be of value to the tribesmen who originally built it? Again, we do not know.

Once the Romans occupied an area, everything changed. We know that they had dealt firmly with the Brigantes by AD 80 and the tribe who lived near Carrock Fell were a junior branch of this greater unity. The Romans encouraged their new subjects to settle in the lower valleys and to supplement their pastoral activities with a little agriculture. A mesh of Roman roads surrounded the Lakeland mountains, and, not so many miles to the north, stood Hadrian's Wall. On a clear day, the people who lived in Carrock Fort – if any of them still used it –

could climb the high fells near them and look down to the shining waters of the Solway Firth and to the 'mile-castles' that lined its banks and continued the protection of the Wall. When the Pictish raiders broke over the Wall, as they did from time to time, did the local tribesmen bring the Carrock Fell Fort back into use?

Not far away, and on the lower ground, lies Caldbeck village. In the churchyard, Britain's most famous fox hunter, John Peel, was buried in 1854. He was born in Green-rigg nearby. No doubt he must have 'oftimes led' his pack, including those hounds celebrated in song, Bellman and True, past Carrock Fell Fort making the ruined walls ring to the sound of his horn!

LEFT: *The crumbled walls of Carrock Fell hill fort*
BELOW: *A sheep pen built from the walls of Carrock Fell hill fort*

STAIGUE FORT, COUNTY KERRY. This is one of the largest and most impressive of the Irish stone forts. It stands at the top of a green, peaceful valley that leads down amongst the grey hills to the waters of the Kenmare inlet on the south-west coast of Ireland. The circular wall stands 18 ft high and the walls are 13 ft thick. The central enclosure is entered through a sort of low tunnel, roofed with slabs, which would be very easy to block against an invader. Once inside you find a series of 'X-shaped' steps leading up to the ramparts. There are two small rooms set in the walls.

Staigue, like Dun Aengus on Inishmore, is a typical stone fort structure – a great wall surrounding a homestead – but its very size suggests that whoever lived here was of more than local importance. Your mind goes back inevitably to Celtic, even to pre-Christian times as you look at it. Did the heroes of the old Irish epics live in such stone forts, for we know that the plan of these buildings was almost unchanged for a thousand years? Although many of the most famous of these folk tales are centred on Ulster you can still picture a great chief like Conchorbar arriving at a fort like Staigue, to be welcomed with feasting and songs from the bards who will tell of the glories of the otherworld that awaits warriors after a noble death in battle.

> Delightful fairy music, travel from one Kingdom to another, drinking mead from bright vessels, talking with one you love.

> We play with men of yellow gold on golden chessboards; we drink clear mead in the company of a proud armed warrior.

The stories that have come down to us depict early Celtic Ireland, in which the ring forts were first developed, as a Homeric society, where the admired virtue is prowess in battle linked with loyalty to the chief or King. The archetype here is Cu Chulainn, who, as Professor Myles Dillon put it, is 'brave, generous, handsome, beloved of women, who chose fame and an early death rather than a long life without honour'. The chariot carries the warrior into battle as it did in Homer's *Iliad*, and the warriors glory in single combat.

We can accept the Irish epics as an accurate picture of life as lived around the old stone forts, for Ireland never came under the yoke of Rome. Until her conversion to Christianity she retained intact the economy, manners and political structure of the ancient Celtic world of the Iron Age. The great swords wielded by Cu Chulainn and his like, the gold torcs that decorated those incomparable beauties Dierdre and Étaín, were forged in a tradition that had continued unbroken from La Tène. True the epics, as we have them today, were written down very much later by monks who might not have been particularly friendly to these pagan survivals. The *Táin Bó Cualnge* (The Cattle Raid of Cooley), the Ulster epic in which Cu Chulainn appears, seems to have been transcribed in the eighth century in the monastery of Bangor, County Down. But we know from classical writers like Caesar, who were fascinated by Celtic life, that memory played a central part in the preservation and transmission of every sort of lore – from judicial decisions to historical details and, above all, epic tales. The *fili* of Ireland seem to have been, as it were, the heirs of the Druids. They preserved the history, the genealogy, the literature handed down to them. Through the carefully cultivated and phenomenal memory of the *fili* the monks were eventually able to put on record the story of Ireland's Celtic past.

LEFT: *Steps up the terraced wall of Staigue Fort and the entrance to the small chamber built within the thickness of the walls*

OVERLEAF: *Staigue Fort in its quiet valley*

GREAT BERNERA, ISLE OF LEWIS, OUTER HEBRIDES. This is an intriguing site, with a mystery attached. In this small loch among the rough, stony hillocks that make up so much of the northern section of the island of Lewis, a causeway leads out over the waters towards a small islet. From low down on the shore the causeway seems complete and tempts you to walk out towards the island. But as you proceed, the stones of the causeway get further apart, and the water around gets deeper until the prudent visitor decides to venture no further and beats a retreat to the shore. On the island there are clearly signs of old dwellings. Why, then, is the causeway made so difficult?

The answer lies in the nature of the causeway. It was constructed on the principle of the 'crannog'. Now a crannog it would appear – like the broch and the dun – is an indigenous British invention which goes back a long way in Ireland and possibly in Scotland, too. The true crannog is a small, artificial island that was constructed by piling up stones on a selected site off shore, until the heap just broke the surface of the water. Then a framework of timber would be laid upon it on which a complex of huts could be raised – which appeared to float upon the water. The crannog-dwellers could reach their artificial island by canoe, or more cunningly, by a twisting causeway which lay just below the normal lake level. Any intruder who ventured out on the causeway would, when reaching one of the twists and gaps – all of which were well known to the natives – slip off into deep water.

The causeway at Great Bernera could hardly lead to a true crannog since the islet out in the lake is not an artificial one. But it can frighten a visitor just the same!

The sunken causeway at Great Bernera

DUN MHUIRICH, STRATHCLYDE. This is a lonely dun, splendidly situated in country where few people come. It is perched on a rocky knoll overlooking the waters of Loch Mhuirich. This is a secluded sea-loch and Dun Mhuirich seems equally secluded. On one side the knoll plunges almost sheer to the sea shore. When you climb up the fairly steep slope to the summit you find that the dun itself is a sort of central keep within an outer wall encircling the upper section of the knoll. The wall of the central section is over 7 ft thick. A dun – pronounced, by the way, 'doon' – was always solidly built which makes the dating of many of them difficult. The original structure may have been abandoned and then reoccupied until late mediaeval times and beyond. But no doubt the original concept must go back to early Pictish times.

That early Pictish invention the 'broch' differed in intent from the 'dun'. The broch was a fortified dwelling place – a strong defensive tower. The dun was slightly less ambitious; it was a high wall encircling the modest buildings of a farming community. No doubt it helped to keep up morale in dangerous times to know that your little farmyard was surrounded by stout walls.

No objects have been found in Dun Mhuirich which might help to date its original construction but there are foundations of later buildings inside the keep. Dun Mhuirich may have had occupants, grateful for the shelter it offered them, until comparatively recent days.

ABOVE: *Man-made fortifications on top of the natural defences at Dun Mhuirich*
RIGHT ABOVE: *View of Loch Mhuirich from within the dun*
RIGHT BELOW: *Looking across the lonely countryside towards the dun*

ABOVE: *Old trees on the way to the 'lost' dun*
RIGHT: *The few remaining stones of the dun*

THE LOST DUN, STRATHCLYDE. Of course this lonely dun near Loch Michaen, in a rarely visited part of Argyll in Scotland's wild west, is not 'lost' in the exact sense of the word. The site is firmly marked on the Ordnance Survey map and it is listed by the archaeologists among the five hundred or more duns that are scattered over west and north-west Scotland. But as you stand amongst the ruins and look towards the waters of the loch, you have a great sense of being lost, not so much in space as in time. The new forests clothe the hills in the distance, a shy deer occasionally disappears across the nearby rocky slope and you wonder who first built these broken walls? How long did they live here? Why did they abandon these fortifications that must have cost them so much labour to construct? The moss-covered stones can give no answer.

There are few duns in this part of the western world which are mentioned by name in the scanty monkish annals and chronicles, passed down to us from this troubled period of Scotland's past. Nevertheless the lonely dun near Loch Michaen must have played its small part in the Irish invasion during the sixth century AD: an invasion which profoundly altered the political structure and even the language of this part of the south-western Highlands. The Scotti were the Ulster tribe who crossed the North Channel, conquered this area from the Picts and eventually gave their name to the whole country. After playing its part our lost dun quietly slipped back into the mists.

LEFT: *Broken walls and a dead tree in a forgotten landscape*

Looking across Thirwall Common; part of Hadrian's wall and the remains of a mile-castle

HADRIAN'S WALL, NORTHUMBERLAND. Hadrian's Wall is the most moving and evocative of all the many remains of the Roman occupation of Britain. You stand on these crags near Housesteads in Northumberland and look away across the bleak country to the north. You are now on the line drawn by the Romans across the neck of Britain to mark the *limes*, the limit of what to them, was civilized Europe. Beyond lay barbarian country, from which danger could come at any moment; wild tribes like the Picts, painted and ruthless, raiding deep into the settled country far to the south. Those living in the snug *colonia* of the South Coast, the retired governors taking the waters at Aquae Sulis (Bath) and the rich merchants trading in Londinium, probably took it all for granted. Rome was the Eternal City; it would last for ever. Hadrian's Wall was the Roman equivalent of Britain's old North-West Frontier in India, but it lasted at least two hundred years longer.

There is no doubt that it was Hadrian, the great consolidator of the Empire, who decided on a powerful stone barrier from the Tyne to the Solway. As has been aptly said, 'he took an engineer's view of the problem'. Augustus had aimed at siting the Roman frontiers along natural barriers like the Rhine. Hadrian felt that these should be supplemented by artificial barriers. The great wall began to rise in the Northumberland wilderness in about AD 122. It was to remain as the great dyke against the rising barbarian flood until the middle of the fourth century.

Along the wall sixteen major forts were constructed. Here the garrisons would live and send out detachments to man the 'mile-castles'. We know where many men of the garrison came from. They included Germans from the Rhineland, Spaniards from the warm south and Celts from Gaul. You sit in the ruined 'mile castles' and wonder how the legionaries felt on duty on the wall on a raw January night, peering into the mists, slapping their chests to stay warm and thinking of a spot of leave in the fleshpots of York.

CARRIGAFOYLE CASTLE, COUNTY KERRY. This lonely tower rises impressively on the flat banks of a tidal inlet in the wide Shannon estuary. The tower has five storeys and is all that remains of a more extensive structure built in the fifteenth or early sixteenth century. It stood originally on an island and was protected by that unique Irish type of defence known as a 'bawn'. A bawn was simply a square courtyard before the main tower, surrounded by a high wall, with small towers at the corners. The bawn could act as a delaying buffer against attack on the main tower. It did not, however, prevent Carrigafoyle repeatedly changing hands during the reign of Elizabeth I when an attempt was made to subdue all Ireland and bring it under English rule.

It was originally built by O'Connor Kerry but, as a native Irish chief, his heirs were bound to choose the weaker side in the long and savage Elizabethan wars. It was taken in 1580 by Sir William Pelham who brought artillery against it. You can still see the large hole blasted by his cannon. Gunfire levelled the whole of the western portion of the castle. Maybe this made it easier for the O'Connor Kerry of the day to retake it. The Irish held it until 1600 when it surrendered again to the English under Sir George Carew. The aging Queen Elizabeth finally granted it to Sir Charles Wilmot.

The castle may soon have a more dangerous enemy to its peace than Sir William Pelham and his great cannon. There is talk of building a big oil terminal near the site.

ABOVE: *One remaining corner of the bawn*

RIGHT: *The ruined western side of the castle*
OVERLEAF: *The Shannon estuary from the high ramparts of the castle*

ABOVE: *Reclaimed marsh land around Carrigafoyle Castle*

MINARD CASTLE, COUNTY KERRY. Minard Castle is an abandoned tower on the southern shores of the Dingle peninsula – the most northerly of the many peninsulas that Ireland thrusts out into the Atlantic from its south-west corner, like the bony fingers of a hand. The peninsula holds the country's second highest mountain, Mount Brandon (3127 ft) and is liberally strewn with a vast variety of antiquities, from megalithic tombs and Celtic beehive huts to castle towers. They all seem to be as splendidly sited as Minard. The Atlantic winds sweep in around it and no woods flourish in that salt-laden air. The scenery around the castle thus has a bare, sparse nobility.

Its history is equally sparse. It was one of the towers of the Knights of Kerry and came to its end in the Irish rising of 1641 that followed the fall of Charles I's great minister, Stafford. As Governor of Ireland he had been efficient, or, as he put it himself 'thorough'. The stage was set for the beginning of the Civil War and inevitably Ireland was drawn in to the conflict. The battle lines were drawn with considerable complexity here in the west. The Catholics, on the whole, were firmly on the side of the King and they were also joined by the 'Old English' gentry, the descendants of the Anglo-Norman invaders. Thus, at Minard in 1641, the 'Old English' Sir Walter Hussey was besieged by the Protestant colonels Helmet and Sadler. In despair, the besieged blew up their own building. Although local legend has it that the attackers, realizing that the defenders had run out of ammunition since they had begun to use pewter shot, laid a charge under one corner of the castle and blew it up.

Minard Castle

Minard Castle is sited in a defensive position on the edge of the Dingle peninsula

CARNASSERIE CASTLE, STRATHCLYDE. This is a rather larger castle than you might expect to find in this south-westerly part of the Scottish Highlands, where the defences run to brochs and isolated hill forts rather than to formal mediaeval castles. But Carnasserie is not so much a castle as a fortified manor house, built in the late sixteenth century by John Carswell, the first Bishop of the Isles after the Scottish Reformation. It symbolizes the unruly spirit of the time, when a bishop had to fortify himself before he could live in his own diocese. The Scottish Reformation came a decade or two after the similar movement in England. Mary, Queen of Scots, a firm Catholic, battled in vain against the Protestants who were inspired by John Knox. Power passed into the hands of the supporters of the Reformed Church but not without strong resistance in the outposts of the Kingdom. To this day many of the Outer Isles remain Catholic.

The strong minded bishop tackled the job of spreading the Gospel according to John Knox with manful determination. He translated Knox's *Liturgy* into Gaelic, the first book to be printed in the Gaelic language. John Carswell's castle-cum-house had a parapet wall and corner towers furnished with gun ports. Perhaps he was uncertain how his flock would react to the Knoxian version of the religion of love for your fellow men and peace on earth?

This interior view of the ground floor of the castle reveals the thickness of the fortifications

ABOVE: *The view from a south-facing window of
Carnasserie Castle*

RIGHT: *Looking west over the remains of the castle*

DUNAMORE CASTLE, CAPE CLEAR ISLAND, COUNTY CORK. This stronghold of the O'Driscoll's stands in a stunningly impressive position on a cliff top on Cape Clear island at the end of the peninsula that runs out into the Atlantic from Skibbereen in the south-west of County Cork. Dunamore means 'golden fort' and perpetuates the story, common to many Irish strongholds in the west, that there is a hoard of gold hidden in the castle.

Cape Clear island is an interesting place. It is the most southerly of all the hundreds of islands off the Irish coast. A few miles out to sea lies the Fastnet Rock, which received worldwide publicity when the yachts in the Fastnet ocean-race came to grief in a furious gale in 1979. The island was the terminus of the early telegraph cable from Ireland to London, and before the first transatlantic cable was laid in 1858, steamers arriving from New York would make their first landfall at Cape Clear. Despatches were thrown overboard in specially marked floating containers. These were retrieved by the local boatmen who brought them back to the island, from where they were swiftly transmitted to London. The arrangement continued even after the laying of the first transatlantic cable.

Cape Clear has always felt a sturdy independence from the mainland. Until the nineteenth century it maintained its own code of law. It is still a strong outpost of the Gaelic language and receives hundreds of language students every summer. On Cape Clear Erse is the first language still, although most 'Capers' are bilingual.

The highest point of the island reaches 440 ft but the coastline is uniformly rocky with high cliffs. Look-outs were built along them after the French expedition to Bantry Bay in 1798, and there is a curious line of upright stones placed along the south-west cliffs. Local tradition maintains that they were painted, and even clothed, in military uniforms to create the impression of a line of soldiers waiting to repel the invaders. The 'Capers' call them *fir breuga* – the false men. The O'Driscolls could have done with a few!

O'BRIEN'S CASTLE, INISHEER, ARAN ISLANDS. A most interesting defensive complex on Inisheer, the smallest of the three inhabited Aran Islands. This was the stronghold of the O'Briens, a Clare family who ruled the islands through the Middle Ages and, due to the position of the Arans in Galway Bay, were able to levy tolls on the trade going into the port of Galway town. They made a very good thing out of it until they were rudely replaced by the O'Flaherty's from Connemara in 1582. The O'Flaherty's had wormed themselves into Queen Elizabeth's good graces, but the O'Briens had the satisfaction of knowing that their supplanters did not last long; royal favour is capricious. In 1587 the Queen handed the lordship of the Arans over to Englishmen. The O'Briens had built their fourteenth century castle in the middle of an ancient ring fort thus proving that the tradition of living in the old style duns was still strong. The ring fort with its mediaeval tower in the centre, surrounded by a maze of limestone walls enclosing small fields, makes an unforgettable impression.

The castle made its final appearance in history during the Civil War and the Cromwellian invasion. The Aran Islands assumed considerable strategic importance since they controlled the approach by sea to Galway town, through which a great deal of outside aid could come to the embattled Irish Catholics. The English navy prevented such aid entering the eastern ports fronting the Irish Sea. The islands changed hands as the fortunes of war turned to one side or the other. The Catholic commander Clanrickarde planned to make the Arans an important base to accommodate the troops and supplies promised him by the Duke of Lorraine. This help never arrived and the Cromwellians seized the islands. Clanrickarde attempted to retake them, but the troops he had landed were forced to surrender in 1652. The O'Brien's Castle (*Furmina* as it is called in Irish) was 'slighted' – blown up and made completely uninhabitable.

A garrison was maintained on the Arans for a considerable time following the Crom-

wellian victory, with interesting results; the 1821 census – the first ever taken on the islands – recorded a surprising number of English names. Goulds, Wilsons, Yorks, Wiggins and Thompsons abound. The proportion has dropped considerably since and the Aran Islanders, whatever the origin of many families may be, are now thoroughly Irish in every way. The Irish language continues to be spoken around the ruined O'Brien castle and the ancient dun before it, as it has been for two thousand years.

ABOVE: *Upturned curraghs on Inisheer beach with O'Brien's castle on the horizon*
LEFT: *The maze of dry stone walls on Inisheer*

LEAMANEH CASTLE, COUNTY CLARE. The first tower was built in 1480 and was slightly in advance of its time for Irish towers; it actually contained small openings for guns. In the first half of the seventeenth century a four-storied mansion was created alongside the tower complete with mullioned windows. The great nobles of England, secure in the domestic peace brought by the Tudors, had started to open up their old mediaeval castles more than 150 years before. The Tudors failed to bring peace to Ireland, and Irish nobles continued to live close in their towers until the later Stuarts brought slightly more settled conditions. Conor O'Brien and his wife Maire Ni Mahon may have thought that by 1643 it was safe to abandon mediaeval towers for modern mansions. If they did so, they were rapidly undeceived.

They had had only a few years to enjoy life in their new Big House when the Cromwellian invasion of Ireland began. Conor

ABOVE: *The original tower can be seen on the right-hand side of the four-storied mansion*

LEFT: *The well worn stairway in the original tower of the castle*

O'Brien naturally supported the Stuarts and fell in battle in a skirmish with the Cromwellian general Ludlow. The story goes that when his strong-minded wife Maire saw the pony carrying his apparently lifeless body approaching the castle she turned it away saying, 'We want no dead men here'. She then saw there was some life left, so she nursed him until he died the same night. Incredibly, she is said to have marched into Limerick next day and married a Cromwellian soldier, Cooper, to keep her son's inheritance in the family. She made up for this, however, by kicking Cooper over the battlements when he was shaving after he had insulted her dead husband's memory. Old Ireland was reputedly a matriarchal society, but Maire Ni Mahon was surely the strongest-minded matriarch of all time!

LEFT: *The floorless interior of Leamaneh Castle. It is from these battlements that Maire Ni Mahon is reputed to have pushed her second husband, Cooper, to his death*

*A break in the cliffs by the castle
complex of Girnigoe and Sinclair
which overlooks the North Sea*

G IRNIGOE AND SINCLAIR CASTLES, WICK. This remarkable castle complex, with two castles rolled into one, stands on the stern coast of Caithness overlooking the North Sea. The site is impressive: the ruins are perched on the cliff edge near a rock tower. Noss Head confronts the dark ocean close to these broken walls, and the sands of Sinclair Bay curve away to the north. The buildings are comparatively late – sixteenth to seventeenth century – but these were still stormy times in Scotland and noblemen, especially in the far north, built their houses for safety rather than elegance. The battle between the supporters of the Reformation, inspired by John Knox and the Catholic rearguard had been fiercely joined. Mary, Queen of Scots, had been driven from her throne after her tempestuous marriage to the ruthless Earl of Bothwell and had gone to her long and eventually fatal captivity in England. The kingdom was being ruled in the name of Mary's infant son, James.

In this troubled political and social atmosphere, men were inclined to use violent solutions to overcome their difficulties. George, 4th Earl of Sinclair, became deeply suspicious of his son, John, whom he accused of plotting his father's death in order to seize the inheritance. He ordered John to be flung into the dungeons in Girnigoe Castle. The unhappy man remained there for seven long years, listening to the wind whistling and the winter seas thundering on the rocks below. No wonder the son eventually died, as the chronicler put it, 'from famine and vermine'.

The black ruins perched on the cliff edge are the perfect setting for so bleak a story.

ABOVE: *The remains of the fallen castles*   RIGHT: *Perched on the cliff edge, a superb defensive position*

CASTLEKIRKE, COUNTY GALWAY. This is, again, a satisfactorily sited castle, built on a small island on Loch Corrib, with the mountains of the west rising behind it. As you row out towards it, the walls seem to rise from the waters. It has a history of sieges, betrayals, wild attacks and desperate defences. The present castle dates from about 1235 and probably replaced an early castle built around 1200 by Roderick O'Connor and Fitzadelm de Burgo. The partnership is an interesting one – an Irishman and an Anglo-Norman combining to build a castle together in the wilds of the old province of Connaught. A decade or two before this first castle on the island was built, Irish history had taken a decisive turn. The death of the great High King, Brian Boru in 1014, had let Ireland in for a century of turmoil, in which the minor kings fought for supremacy. At last, Dermot MacMurrough of Munster invited over the Anglo-Normans under Strongbow.

The newcomers brought with them new methods of castle building. In the first stage of the conquest they held down the land they had won with easily constructed 'motte and bailey' type fortifications. But by 1200 they were turning to more permanent stone structures. More interesting still, the Anglo-Norman invaders were becoming more Irish than the Irish. They rapidly intermarried with the native dynasties and immersed themselves in the complicated internal politics of Ireland. It is thus no surprise to find that Roderick O'Connor turned to Fitzadelm de Burgo when he set about building this first Castlekirke. Many Irish chieftains were slow to adopt the new technique, but the O'Connors of Connaught had succeeded in keeping most of their territory intact and moved with the times. Their castle on the island was rectangular and was impressive for the west of Ireland. Rebuilt in 1233 and again by Fedlim, King of Connaught, it was destroyed by the English under Cromwell.

LEFT: *The remains of Castlekirke*
OVERLEAF: *The head of Loch Corrib and, in the distance, the small island on which the castle stands*
FOLLOWING PAGES: *A closer view of the island*

CLIFDEN CASTLE, COUNTY GALWAY. Ireland has a long tradition of creating ruins and it is hardly her fault. Each unhappy period added its own quota. Henry VIII put paid to many of the abbeys and priories and the Elizabethan wars added to the destruction. Cromwell 'slighted' the castles and dealt with those abbeys that had escaped Henry. The 'Troubles' after the First World War added their quota of burnt-out 'great houses'. Swiftly the consoling green has covered them all and softened the scars. Thus the old abandoned mansion of Clifden has now taken on the charm of a genuine Gothic castle.

This mock Gothic fantasy was built by John D'Arcy, who was the great-nephew of Count Patrick D'Arsy (or D'Orsey), 1725–89, one of those remarkable foreigners who settled in Ireland and became 'more Irish than the Irish'. He was a Jacobite, a soldier, a scientist and a Member of the French Academy. His great-nephew inherited his creative urge; he founded Clifden in 1812 as a new town and port in order to develop this previously neglected part of the country. His 'castle' lies about a mile and a half outside the town in the midst of splendid scenery. Not many miles away are the Twelve Bens of Connemara with their challenge to the mountain walker, and the sea coast is splendid. Clifden itself is now a friendly, flourishing little market-town.

The only time it attracted world attention was on 18 June 1919. On that memorable day the Handley-Page bomber carrying John Alcock and Arthur Whitten Brown passed over Clifden Castle and town as the pilots looked desperately for a landing place. They had just made landfall, with their fuel running low, after making the first West–East flight by a powered aircraft across the Atlantic. They had a soft landing in a bog five miles beyond Clifden. This was fortunate; the landscape around Clifden is extremely rocky in parts. There is a cairn marking the landing place and a monument on firmer ground a mile or so away.

R AHINNANE CASTLE, COUNTY KERRY. This
is one of the many castles, or rather castle towers, built by the Knights of Kerry in
the Dingle peninsula and in their other Kerry territories. Here in the far west, there was
not much money available for elaborate
constructions. They simply wanted safe tem-
porary refuge in troubled times, and in the
west, all times seem to have been troubled.

The castle, however, is a sturdy, thick-
walled two storied affair with some unusual
arcaded construction on the ceiling of the
second floor. It has the remains of a few out-
buildings near at hand and stands in the middle of a wide circular area marked by a ditch
which is 30 ft deep in places. This must be
the remains of a far earlier fortification,
perhaps an old ring fort or even a Bronze
Age defence work. The same sites were
occupied again and again in Irish history.

The castle inevitably came under repeated
attack as the English rulers began their policy
of 'planting' Irish territories with English,
Scottish or Welsh settlers. The 'plantation'
policy was strongly pursued under Mary
Tudor and Elizabeth. The plantation of
Ulster was a success from the English point
of view if not from the Irish. Irish resistance
rendered the plantation of Munster less
complete. But Rahinnane Castle was taken
by Sir Charles Wilmot in 1603, and was
finally 'slighted' and destroyed during the
Cromwellian wars fifty years later.

KILCOE CASTLE, COUNTY CORK. A beautifully placed double tower, on a small islet connected by a causeway to the mainland in the expressively named Roaringwater Bay. These lonely strongholds of south-west Ireland have a strong romantic appeal, and it is not surprising that Kilcoe is privately owned and that the new owners might even consider living in it themselves.

These castles of the west were, perhaps, too grandiosely named; they were more like the pele-towers on the English-Scottish border. In the more fertile eastern counties of Ireland, however, great castles in the approved concentric style were still built. The remains of Trim Castle in County Meath on the banks of the Boyne are as impressive as Conway or Caerphilly. There was no money out west to construct castles like Trim.

No matter. Hospitality was a great tradition and even the humblest castle gave the traveller a heartwarming welcome. Another early seventeenth-century traveller, Luke Gernon, left a delightful description of his reception at a castle which must have been similar to Kilcoe. The lady of the house met the visitor, accompanied by the servants.

> Salutations past, you shall be presented with all the drinks in the house, first the ordinary beer, then aquavitae, then old-ale. The lady tastes it, you must not refuse it. The fire is prepared in the middle of the hall, where you may solace yourself 'til supper time, you shall not want sack and tobacco. By this time the table is spread and plentifully furnished with variety of meats, but ill-cooked and without sauce.

But the cooking hardly mattered in the middle of general jollity and singing with the harper playing away like mad. In the morning, you were offered whiskey when you got up. 'It is a very wholesome drink,' Luke Gernon hastens to tell us, 'and natural to digest the crudities of Irish feeding.' More drinks at the door on departure. Luke Gernon's advice: 'smack them over and depart.' That is, if you can!

WORKING PLACES

Forget six counties over-hung by smoke,
Forget the snorting steam and piston stroke,
Forget the spreading of the hideous town,
Think rather of the pack-horse on the down . .

WILLIAM MORRIS

THE KILLHOPE WHEEL, COUNTY DURHAM

GREENBURN BECK LEAD MINE, CUMBRIA

OLD COKE OVENS, COUNTY DURHAM

ABEREIDDI BAY, DYFED

THE LOST CARRIAGE, NEAR CHESTERS,
NORTHUMBERLAND

OLD GANG SMELT MILL, SWALEDALE,
YORKSHIRE

THE DESERTED JETTY, INISHEER, ARAN ISLANDS

CHARCOAL BURNING SITE, NEWBY BRIDGE,
LAKE DISTRICT

PARYS MOUNTIAN, ANGLESEY, GWYNEDD

THE STRANDED COASTER, INISHEER, ARAN
ISLANDS

POWDER MILLS, DARTMOOR, DEVON

The remains of a coke oven at
Inkerman, County Durham

THE KILLHOPE WHEEL, COUNTY DURHAM.
A new fashion in secret landscapes has
attracted the general public in recent years;
industrial archaeologists have made us aware
of the fascination and importance of the
ruins of the places where our forefathers
once worked. Here they fashioned the techniques of the Industrial Revolution of the
eighteenth century which laid the foundation of the way in which we now live. Between us and the age of the Stuarts lies more
than 250 years of continuous invention; of
growing cities and of ever increasing mobil-

ity for the Common Man. There is something profoundly moving about the workplaces where men once laboured, in hard relentless conditions, and which now lie lost and silent in areas where few people come. We live as we do because of the work our forefathers did in places like Killhope.

The great steel wheel was used to power a crushing plant for the ores brought down from the lead mines in Upper Weardale. The mines were opened in the eighteenth century and continued working until around 1860. The steam engine would have been out of

ABOVE: *Wreathed in mist the wheel at Killhope and behind it the crushing plant*
LEFT: *The great steel wheel*

place and uneconomic among these hills where water power was available almost free on the spot. The lead that buttressed the Industrial Revolution was basically home-produced, but by the end of the nineteenth century, new sources of supply were being opened up around the world. Slowly the busy sound of the ore crushers faded. The great wheels ceased to turn. Silence returned to the hills.

G REENBURN BECK LEAD MINE, CUMBRIA.
Lead mines seem to supply most of the romantic ruins among our mountains. Slate quarries are the only other industrial activity that invades the high hills on a big scale, but truth to tell, quarries seem more in tune with the landscape when they are abandoned than when they are in full working order. They can expand on too big a scale for visual comfort; indeed, they can form secret landscapes on their own.

Lead mines, in their old age, are kinder to the hills. They fade back gracefully into the countryside although, alas, it takes many years before the mountain streams rid themselves of the 'tailing' that kills the trout.

These mines in the Lake District lie in one of the less visited parts – if one can say that about any section of crowded Cumbria in the holiday season. The Ulpha Fells run southwards from that great knot of crags that cluster around Scafell Pike to form the highest point of England. They also look eastwards across the valley of the River Duddon to where the rugged Old Man of Coniston presides over the long Coniston Water. Unspoilt country, through which that remorseless pedestrian, the poet Wordsworth, marched composing an equally pedestrian series of sonnets on his way. He described the Duddon as

Child of the clouds! remote from every
    taint
Of sordid industry thy lot is cast;

While Wordsworth was busy composing his poem, a group of keen businessmen were equally busy composing the prospectus of the Greenburn Beck Leadmining Company. Wordsworth, who was naturally not consulted about the terms of the prospectus, described this stern country as composed of 'unfruitful solitudes, that seem to upbraid, The sun in heaven!' The lead miners opened up lodes that, for a short time, proved anything but unfruitful! 'Sordid industry' came for a brief spell to Ulpha Fell.

Lead is not easy to mine; the ore lies in lodes that twine and twist among the rocks.

Lead miners have none of the certainty of operation that coal miners have. A coal measure can be thrown by a fault, but on the whole it runs reasonably level. Lead gives the impression that it was poured haphazardly

among the cracks in the most ancient rocks of Britain. The ore on Ulpha Fell eventually proved uneconomic and too difficult to work and the area has returned to unfruitful but happy solitude.

OLD COKE OVENS, COUNTY DURHAM. These intriguing structures are found on the western edge of the Durham coalfield at Inkerman, a name that recalls the Crimean War. At first glance these circular buildings look like the old beehive huts of the early Irish monks, with the top sliced off. Actually they are coke ovens, dating from the early days of the Industrial Revolution. These particular ovens were closed and abandoned in the early nineteenth century after perhaps fifty years of vigorous and important industrial life.

The famous iron-master Abraham Derby first recognized the importance of coke when he perfected his process of iron smelting with it around 1707. It was a turning point in the iron business since it removed it, as one distinguished industrial historian said, 'from the tyranny of wood and water'. Until Abraham Derby showed the way, iron smelting depended on the production of charcoal from the steadily diminishing tim-

ber resources of places like the Sussex Weald. After the turn of the eighteenth century charcoal faded, to be replaced by coke produced from beehive-type ovens like those at Inkerman.

The technique was basically simple but demanded care. The coal was loaded into the beehive oven through a hole in its base and a draught was created to burn the coal at a controlled rate, the fumes escaping through the aperture at the top of the oven. The power of the draught was controlled by nar-

rowing the hole through which the coal was loaded with bricks or clay. This enabled air to pass through the oven; a fire which burnt too fast reduced the coal to useless ashes.

Certain coals were better for coking than others, but all coalfields, including Durham, produced acceptable coking coals. There was no problem in feeding the furnaces at Inkerman, until the old beehive ovens became an industrial curiosity in the 1850s.

ABOVE: *The ovens were abandoned early in the nineteenth century*
LEFT: *From a distance these two ovens at Inkerman look like beehives*

ABEREIDDI BAY, DYFED. Romantic industrial ruins are not the sole property of the mountain country. The coastline can also offer surprises and delights to the industrial archaeologist. At Abereiddi, a small hamlet on the coast of northern Pembrokeshire (Dyfed) a slate quarry was opened in the late nineteenth century. The Ordovician shales here have been subjected to intense pressure in past ages and cleave easily as a result. This vein of slate crops up again in Pembrokeshire on the Presely Hills at Rosebush and near Maenclochog, whence came the slates that were chosen to roof the new Houses of Parliament at Westminster.

The Abereiddi slates were also of high quality and were exported from the tiny harbour of Porthgain, a mile or so to the north. The two places were connected by a tramroad. The trade attracted North Wales quarrymen to Abereiddi and, in the heyday of the industry – when the big industrial towns were expanding – Pembrokeshire slate was in great demand. Abereiddi helped to roof thousands of 'Coronation Streets'. But eventually the great Caernarvonshire (Gwynedd) quarries proved too efficient and

slates ceased to be quarried at Abereiddi in 1904. Porthgain continued to export crushed stone until it, too, closed in 1931.

But the workings have left a place of strange beauty in Abereiddi. A great hollow has been carved out of the cliff edge, with a narrow entrance to the sea. In a curious way, it looks like a miniature Lulworth Cove and, inevitably, it has been christened the 'Blue Lagoon'. The Pembrokeshire Path passes along its edge near the guardian tower. To the south stretch the curious dark sands of Abereiddi Bay. The sea tends to wear back the shale here and some of the old fishermen's cottages have had to be abandoned. But there is a compensation for geologists; the shales at Abereiddi are rich in certain types of fossils. Triolobites are one variety to be found there, but the chief prizes are the grapholites, known as tuning-fork grapholites from their strange shape.

ABOVE: *The edge of the slate quarry and the inlet formed by the quarrying operations*
LEFT: *The peculiar islet formed in Abereiddi Bay by the quarrying*

THE LOST CARRIAGE, NEAR CHESTERS, NORTHUMBERLAND. Beside the path that leads to the Chesters Roman bridge abutment, Michael Hales caught sight of a strangely elegant structure under the trees on the edge of a wood. What could it be? A Regency 'cottage orné' complete with balcony? The beams of an ancient ruined tithe-barn? The wooden framework had a certain picturesque charm which seemed to demand a camera shot. A closer look disclosed nothing more romantic than an old railway carriage, with only its framework left! But it had set a train of thought going. Here, lost in the countryside, was a memorial to the great Age of Steam, the 170 year reign of the steam locomotive which came to an end a mere twenty years ago when British Rail went over to diesel traction and sent the great steam engines to puff away and die in the graveyard of steam at Barry in South Wales.

There is a sad irony in this for only twenty-five miles from Barry, is the railway track from Merthyr to Abercynon down which the Cornishman, Richard Trevethick drove the first steam train in the world in 1804. His engine had the firebox in front and he ran alongside stoking it, as it raced ahead at a dizzy five miles an hour. No matter! He completed the journey, with his engine drawing a string of heavy trams on which rode seventy jubilant passengers. It was the start of a new era. Poor old Trevethick made nothing out of it. The next engine he built, after his South Wales triumph, became a sort of peep-show in London. You paid one shilling to see the 'Catch-me-if-you-can' puff around an enclosure in Torrington Square. Not far away was the site on which Euston Station was shortly to rise. One hundred and forty years later, that masterpiece of steam locomotion, 'Mallard', drew a train at a world record 126 miles an hour!

This old carriage was hardly likely to have been drawn by 'Mallard', but it might have been attached to one of the rival engines that competed in the 'Race to the North' in the 1890s, when the companies put everything into being the fastest into Aberdeen.

OLD GANG SMELT MILL, SWALEDALE, YORKSHIRE. The search for minerals took the miners into the wilder and more beautiful parts of the country. Old Gang Smelt Mill lies in the lonely mountain cleft called Hard Level Gill, which tumbles in little waterfalls down to meet the wider Swaledale beyond Reeth and Healaugh. Swaledale continues on under the delightfully named fell of Lovely Seat. These Pennine moorlands, however, may not have seemed so lovely to the first prospectors who came up into the hills!

It is probable that the first miners could have been the Romans. The Empire was centred around the Mediterranean, where the recent Tertiary rocks are not noticeably rich in minerals. The Imperial structure needed lead, copper, silver and gold to maintain its imposing façade, so behind the legions marched the miners and prospectors. Lowland Britain was occupied by AD 50. It was rich in grain but still poor in minerals. Thirty years later the legions surged on into the west and north, driven by two motives: they had to subdue the dangerous hill tribes who menaced the placid lowlands, and they desperately needed the minerals that lay in places like Hard Level Gill.

The eighteenth-century miners who followed them were driven by the same need; the Industrial Revolution was in full swing and British ores were in demand. It paid to build a smelt mill up in this wilderness,

although getting fuel for the furnaces posed a problem. It would have been uneconomic to import coal and the forests had long since been cleared in Swaledale. The smelters naturally turned to the nearby deposits of peat. Among the ruins of the furnace house, the stores and the blacksmith's shop are the stumpy foundations of a big peathouse. It was 4000 ft long and could hold a year's supply of peat to feed the furnace. The demand for home-produced lead, however, ran out before the supply of peat.

ABOVE LEFT: *These columns are all that remain of the peat storage building*
ABOVE: *The ruined furnace house*
OVERLEAF: *The entrance to a lead mine near the Old Gang Smelt Mill*

THE DESERTED JETTY, INISHEER, ARAN ISLANDS. A concrete slipway runs down to the sea over the great limestone boulders that form the coastline on this part of Inisheer, the smallest inhabited island of the Aran group. The hills of the mainland, around Galway Bay, show in the distance. The little jetty seems deserted; its only occupants a congregation of cormorants. They look like a group of Welsh deacons discussing the sermon after chapel, or rather – as this is a staunchly Catholic island – like a Sunday procession of Jesuit seminarists in black soutanes!

No doubt this causeway was built under one of the many schemes promoted by governments, English and Irish, over the last hundred years to bring some kind of prosperity to the rugged western regions of Ireland. Piers and jetties were a favourite panacea for many of the troubles of the Gaeltacht. When J. M. Synge stayed in Inishmaan to learn Erse at the beginning of the twentieth century, the life of the islanders was certainly more self-contained than it is today. The Congested Districts Board, set up in 1891, had already built the inevitable pier at Kilronan on Inishmore, but most of the islanders lived close to subsistence level. They needed the harvest of the sea to supplement the meagre harvest of the land.

Synge fashioned his own language out of the Erse spoken on Aran. Probably no islander ever expressed himself like a character in a Synge play, but this doesn't matter. He caught the essential spirit of the place. Much has changed in our own day, and the visitor must not expect the islanders to look and behave as they do in Robert Flaherty's film *Man of Aran*. But if you walk down this jetty – and disturb the cormorants – you will sense the link that still ties Aran unbreakably to the sea – to its bounty and to its cruelty.

CHARCOAL BURNING SITE, NEWBY BRIDGE, LAKE DISTRICT. Newby Bridge is a pretty village on the River Leven, near the point where it flows out of the southern end of Lake Windermere. To the west lies tumbled, wooded country which leads down to the Furness peninsula. Until the seventeenth century the Furness forest was one of the important industrial areas of Britain; here charcoal-burners and iron-smelters worked together, since charcoal was the only acceptable fuel for the portable iron forges. The owners of a large part of the Furness area were the monks of Cartmel Priory who made a good thing out of the charcoal burning rights, although the iron workers were subject to raids by marauding Scots who carried off ore and water-powered bellows in what might be regarded as early 'take-over bids'.

By Stuart times the charcoal-burners had made such inroads into the forest that even the scrubland on the edge of the moors, like this site at Rusland, was being pressed into service. Once Abraham Derby had developed his coal smelting process early in the eighteenth century there was no further need for Rusland and the rest of the charcoal-burning sites.

PARYS MOUNTAIN, ANGLESEY, GWYNEDD. Behind the little town of Amlwch, where now the great oil tankers anchor to unload, lies a strange tumbled area of deep pits and tips which looks like the outpouring of a volcanic eruption. This is the once world famous copper mine of Parys Mountain. Over it stands the gaunt tower of the windmill that powered the pumps, as a memorial to the organizing genius who, by 1787, had succeeded in dominating the copper trade of the whole world.

Copper was discovered on Parys Mountain in 1768 and the ore proved to be enormously rich. The first discoverer received a small pension and a permanent cottage at the foot of the mountain. The landowners became happier still when they brought in the local solicitor, Thomas Williams, to control the business. He undercut the Cornish producers, pioneered copper-sheathing and bolts for ships and built new smelting works at Swansea. He knew it was cheaper to take the ore to the coal and not bring the coal to Anglesey. Parys Mountain was one of the show places of the Industrial Revolution, but by the time Williams died in 1802 the ore was already becoming exhausted.

The mine buildings and tips at Parys Mountain

THE STRANDED COASTER, INISHEER, ARAN ISLANDS. There is something monstrous and unnatural about a ship cast up almost intact and stranded on a rocky shore. It has no real right to be there; a ship is designed for movement. Even when it is tied up in harbour you sense in it a desire to be quit of the land, to float free on the ocean for which it was created. It is stranger still when a ship stranded over sixty years ago still remains on the spot on which it went aground. This is what happened to the coaster *Plassey* which went ashore in 1916 on Inisheer. There are two powerful lights on the Arans as well as two lesser ones and between them they define the length of the islands. It was wartime, however, and navigation around the complex western coast of Ireland was rendered doubly difficult by the lack of leading marks and lights; once the submarine menace had become acute, the lights had been concealed. It is difficult to blame the *Plassey*'s skipper for going astray in such conditions; he would probably prefer to be wrecked rather than torpedoed.

The west coast of Ireland, in any case, has always had a reputation for disaster among sailors. Perhaps it dates from the agony of the ships of the Spanish Armada in that stormy September when 'the Most Fortunate Fleet' had struggled to get home to Spain by sailing around Scotland and Ireland. Few of the captains had charts; after their defeat in the Channel there had been no chance to repair broken spars and torn sails. Continuous gales pursued them from the moment they sighted the Irish coast and great ships were cast away down the whole length of it. We know that the galleon of Don Luis de Cordoba limped into Galway for shelter, her torn sails carrying her past the very spot where the *Plassey* is now stranded on Inisheer. He received a cold reception: his crew were too weak to man the capstan to warp the galleon out to sea again and they were stripped of their gold and all killed.

After a story like that, the *Plassey*, rusting away on her permanent resting place on the patterned, limestone rocks of Inisheer, seems almost a happy little shipwreck!

The Plassey *stranded on Inisheer's inhospitable shore*

POWDER MILLS, DARTMOOR, DEVON. To this day the people who make and handle high explosives inherit a certain mystic aura from the past. Most of us have no personal experience of such dangerous material. When gunpowder first appeared in the Middle Ages, the master-gunners were a race apart; practitioners of an art inherited from the Devil! The mystique of high explosives is increased by the isolation demanded by the manufacturing process; no one wants to live next door to a powder factory. When demand grew in the nineteenth century for 'rock powder' in the slate and granite quarries of the West Country, it was natural that a powder factory should be established in a then remote part of Dartmoor, Cherrybrook, between Two Bridges and Postbridge. These powder mills flourished there for fifty years. Trees were planted around the gunpowder huts in the hope of minimizing the effects of an explosion, although an explosion in 1858 did £500 worth of damage.

The presiding genius of the enterprise in the mid-nineteenth century was Plymouth alderman, George Frean. He used methods perfected in Royal Ordnance factories, mixing charcoal with saltpetre and sulphur and then grinding the powder in a stone trough using huge stone wheels, driven by water power from the East Dart river. The powder was tested on the spot by firing an iron ball from a mortar; quality was judged by the distance the ball travelled. The Dartmoor powder mills flourished until newer, more effective and less temperamental explosives replaced gunpowder. In the 1890s the establishment, which had employed one hundred men, closed. A farm now occupies the site. The mortar-testing position can still be seen, but the leat that supplied the water is long since dry.

These remains of the small buildings of the Dartmoor powder mills are where the grinding operations took place

PLACES OF PAGAN WORSHIP

Speak Thou, whose massey strength and
stature scorn
The power of years – pre-eminent, and placed
Apart to overlook the circle vast –
Speak, Giant Mother!
WILLIAM WORDSWORTH

KINTRAW STANDING STONE, STRATHCLYDE

CASTLERIGG STONE CIRCLE, CUMBRIA

THE RING OF BRODGAR, ORKNEY ISLANDS

STENNESS HENGE AND STANDING STONE,
ORKNEY ISLANDS

CALLANISH STANDING STONE, ISLE OF LEWIS,
OUTER HEBRIDES

ACHNABRECK CUP-AND-RING MARKINGS,
STRATHCLYDE

CARN MEINI, DYFED

Central stones of Callanish standing stones, Isle of Lewis, Outer Hebrides

KINTRAW STANDING STONE, STRATHCLYDE. 'Speak, Giant Mother!' Wordsworth demanded of the great standing stone called Long Meg, which stands on the edge of one of the most impressive stone circles in Cumbria. He would probably have made the same request to the finely placed standing stone at Kintraw near the head of Loch Craignish. This strange shaft of granite is surrounded by burial cairns; all around lies a lonely, mountainous landscape. We look with awe at this 13 ft high stone and are compelled to ask why the builders of the cairns placed it here – if indeed the men who built the cairns and those who raised the standing stone at Kintraw were one and the same people.

'Giant Mother' Wordsworth called Long Meg; a lucky anticipation of later archaeological theories which suggested that standing stones were linked with the imported cult of the old Mediterranean Mother-Goddess. The great stones, and the stone circles that often lie near them, have not yet given a real answer to our questions although archaeologists have been struggling to make them speak for the past 250 years.

The earlier speculators assigned them to a whole series of ancient heroes from Julius Caesar to King Arthur and his knights; by the eighteenth century the Druids had become the favoured candidates. But the stones still bemuse certain people in the twentieth century. New scientific methods such as radiocarbon dating have now come to the aid of the inquirer and allow the specialist to do much more than simply guess the age of these strangely compelling monuments. Yet as Aubrey Burl points out in the first complete survey of the stone circles of Britain, they remain enigmas. 'They are still unclassified while chambered tombs, hill-forts, barrows, henges, causewayed enclosures and settlements have been excavated, catalogued and analysed.' The standing stones and the stone circles are thus a happy hunting ground for the amateur theorist.

CASTLERIGG STONE CIRCLE, CUMBRIA. This well known circle is splendidly placed. All around are the Lakeland fells and as you stand in the centre of the circle, you see the changing pattern made by the clouds over the high hills. Surely, the people who placed these grey stones in position with so much labour must have felt the awesome beauty of this place; its loneliness and its grandeur. But what do we really know about the builders of Castlerigg and the motives that drove them to plan this strange circle among the mountains?

Certain facts are emerging from modern studies of the stone circles of Britain. First, about 900 of them, of various shapes and sizes; have been recorded. There might have been many more originally, but some have been destroyed within living memory; indeed the vandalism has continued into our own day. Quite recently a circle in South Wales at Pen-y-Beacon – a site as lonely as Castlerigg – was converted into a car park! However, enough remain for us to feel that they are part of our national heritage and should be carefully guarded.

Secondly, the modern method of carbon-14 dating has been applied to organic material found in the circles and has revealed the period during which most of the circles were constructed. The earliest date comes from New Grange in Eire, the latest from the Sandy Road circle at Scone in Scotland; thus we know that circle building extended from about 3300 BC to 1500 BC. An intriguing fact that emerges from the dating process is that Stonehenge comes very late in the series; Castlerigg was constructed many centuries earlier. Stonehenge, it would seem, is the sophisticated climax of 2000 years of endeavour.

Thirdly, even allowing for all the circles that have been destroyed, the number of circles shows an average rate of construction of two a year. As Burl has pointed out, this hardly indicates – as some have maintained – that they were inspired 'by zealots and proselyzing missionaries advocating a crash programme of building in order to observe the next lunar eclipse'.

THE RING OF BRODGAR, ORKNEY ISLANDS. Within a circular bank 120 yards in diameter stand twenty-seven thin, elegant stones, the tallest reaching 15 ft. The Ring is deeply impressive when seen under dark skies with the waters of Loch Stenness and Loch Harray nearby. The Ring of Brodgar stands on one side of the narrow isthmus formed by these two lochs with the Stenness Circle on the other. This narrow neck of land may have formed a boundary between two separate social areas. The whole area is rich in megalithic monuments. Not very far away is the great tomb of Maes Howe, which has been described as 'one of the most awe-inspiring monuments in Europe'. The Ring of Brodgar has inspired awe in all its visitors: the Vikings came in the ninth century and left twenty-four runic inscriptions on its stones; early Irish travellers must have come to admire it as well, for they left a memorial of their presence in ogam marks on four of the stones. Ogam is a curious script, developed in Ireland around the beginning of the Christian era, in which the letters are indicated by strokes cut on either side of a line or the edge of a stone.

Unfortunately the builders of the Ring, sometime in the second millennium BC had no script, and therefore have left us no direct indication of their reasons for placing the great, grey stones against the dark Orcadian sky. As at Callanish and nearby Stenness, Professor Thom and the supporters of the astronomical origins of the stone circles have found precise alignments for certain stones. They claim that the site is lunar oriented and was chosen because it gives three certain indications of the position of the moon. It is hard not to agree that these circles must have had some astronomical significance.

But are stone circles such exact observatories? It is this exactness that Professor Thom's opponents find hard to swallow. Surely the circles must also have had some social significance as places where men would come together regularly for lawmaking and religious ceremonies? The average visitor will leave the arguments to the experts and just stand and admire.

Silhouetted against the sky the Ring of Brodgar leaves a lasting impression on all who visit it

STENNESS HENGE AND STANDING STONES, ORKNEY ISLANDS. The Ring of Stenness stands in bleak, treeless, windswept country on the largest of the Orkney Islands, Mainland. There are four tall stones and the remains of a circle set inside a wide circular bank or ditch. The so-called 'dolmen' standing within the circle is a modern addition dating from 1908 when some of the fallen stones were put together in what the 'restorers' thought, for some unexplained reason, was their original structure. This must have been an important centre for the circle-builders, for not so far away is the tall Watch Stone which may have been part of an avenue linking the Stenness monument with the even more impressive Ring of Brodgar.

The inhabitants have changed often in the remote Orkneys. In the last invasion of historic times, the Norsemen dispossessed the Picts. But this is recent history: we may never know who actually built Stenness 3000 or perhaps 4000 years ago; yet somehow the feeling that this was a particularly holy and powerful place has persisted through the ages. Martin Martin, whose *Description of the Western Isles* so delighted Dr Johnson, reported that, as late as the seventeenth century, the Orcadians believed that Brodgar and Stenness were temples of the sun and moon. They retained a traditional belief that pagan sacrifices were performed there: those to the sun took place in Brodgar; those to the moon took place in the smaller circle of Stenness.

Two great pillars of the Stenness monument are supposed to wrench themselves from their base at midnight on New Year's Eve and roll down to the sea to bathe. After this ceremony they return to their accustomed place. An intriguing story, and one told about other standing stones and cromlechs. Far away, in the Gower peninsula, South Wales, the huge capstone of Arthur's Stone was believed to go down to the Loughor estuary and drink on New Year's Eve. Perhaps these legends reflect the fact that so many of these bigger circles all stand so close to the sea.

The people who built them would naturally have travelled by sea especially in northern and western Scotland. Travelling in the interior among wild mountains covered with forests would have been dangerous and impracticable. There was clearly an accepted route leading from Cumbria over to Ireland and then, up through the inner isles, avoiding such dangerous traps as the notorious whirlpool of Corryvreckan, the Scottish Maelstrom, between Scarba and the northern end of Jura. Did the ideas that led to the building of these great monuments travel northwards along this route or did they perhaps arise independently from local needs?

RIGHT: *Above the bleak landscape stand the stones of Stenness*
OVERLEAF: *The four remaining stones of Stenness looking towards Stromness*

CALLANISH STANDING STONES, ISLE OF LEWIS, OUTER HEBRIDES. This remarkable assembly of tall, thin standing stones is set in a circle and surrounds a central stone beside a chambered cairn. Together with its attendant stone avenues it forms one of the most impressive archaeological spectacles in Britain. The setting is close to the sea, and once again the questions crowd in on us: who built it and for what purpose?

Alexander Thom has no doubts about the purpose; he sees it as a sophisticated celestial observatory. He has made careful measurements, not only of Callanish, but of 200

other sites in Britain. As a result, he claims that the builders of all these circles had a standard unit of measurement, which he calls the 'Megalithic Yard'. This allowed them to construct not just perfect circles but ovoids, egg-shaped and elliptical circles as required for special observations. His oppo-nents, and they are many, point out that the idea of the 'Megalithic Yard' inevitably brings in its train the supposition that there was an intellectual élite capable of enforcing it. Was the primitive agricultural structure of Britain 4000 or 5000 years ago capable of supporting a uniform political unit?

ACHNABRECK CUP-AND-RING MARKINGS, STRATHCLYDE. Scattered throughout Britain and Ireland are curious ornamentations on rock faces, standing stones and ceremonial places. Here on the rocks at Achnabreck, near Lochgilphead, is one of the largest group of these rock carvings known in Britain. The inscribed markings consist of cups and rings, one cup having as many as seven rings; a double spiral occurs on the upper rock face. The designs seem to have been made with a pick or hammered out with a punch. The cups are shallow and so clearly could not have been intended to hold water. The Achnabreck markings occur on a bare rock face, but similar designs have been inscribed on slabs in tombs or on stones in circles.

One suggestion connects the cup and ring motif to the well known Mediterranean labyrinth design; another suggestion is that it could be a formalized representation of the sun as the source of heat and life. Some of the Irish tombs have similar decorations.

Such decorations take a great deal of labour to inscribe so they must have had some vital significance for the people who made them. Perhaps they were magical signs used by the copper prospectors and miners in the second millennium BC. We simply cannot be certain; it is this mystery that makes them so fascinating!

CARN MEINI, DYFED. Carn Meini is a rocky outcrop on the magical Presely Hills in the northern section of the old county of Pembrokeshire (now Dyfed). The highest point of the Preselys passes the 1700 ft mark, but height has nothing to do with the impression that these unspoilt moorlands make on those who walk the ancient trackway that runs their whole length. Strange outcrops of ancient granite break through the bracken and heather, like the tors of Dartmoor. Cromlechs, burial chambers and lost stone circles litter the hillsides. Clearly this was an area of vital importance to the people who built the great megalithic monuments of Britain 4000 years ago.

In 1923 Dr H. H. Thomas startled the archaeological world by proving that the blue stones in the inner circle of Stonehenge were geologically composed of a spotted dolerite formation which only occurs in Britain on Carn Meini and adjacent outcrops on the Preselys. To get them to Stonehenge, devoted men must have ferried them on rafts down to Milford Haven and then up the Bristol Channel to the Avon. From this river, they were dragged over the chalk downs of Wiltshire to Salisbury Plain. Bluestones still lie unmoved on Carn Meini.

ABOVE: *The rocky outcrop of Carn Meini stands out on the horizon*
OVERLEAF: *A tumbled heap of dolerite slabs on Carn Meini*

THE COMING OF CHRISTIANITY

Bare ruined choirs where late the sweet birds sang

WILLIAM SHAKESPEARE

SKELLIG MICHAEL, COUNTY KERRY

SHERKIN MONASTERY, COUNTY CORK

KNOWLTON CHURCH, DORSET

GALLARUS ORATORY, COUNTY KERRY

THE MADONNA OF VALENCIA ISLAND, COUNTY KERRY

IONA ISLAND, STRATHCLYDE

THE SEVEN CHURCHES, INISHMORE, ARAN ISLANDS

CORCOMROE ABBEY, COUNTY CLARE

INISHCALTRA, COUNTY CLARE

Cells of the monastery of Skellig Michael

S KELLIG MICHAEL, COUNTY KERRY. 'The most remote outpost of Christ's Kingdom in the Western World.' This collection of beehive huts around a tiny boat-shaped oratory clings precariously to the summit rocks on the largest of two wild islets, seven miles out into the Atlantic, off Bolus Head on Ireland's savage south-west coast. The largest island is dedicated to St Michael, the patron saint of high places, and as you climb up the rickety stairway of stone slabs leading up amongst the rocks, that plunge steeply into the sea, you feel the need of the Saint's aid at every step. What profound faith must have moved the old Celtic monks to row out over the waves and settle here among the screaming sea-birds in the seventh century. What a life of dedicated prayer they must have lived in their six tiny cells near the burial plot, artificially created by carrying up soil from the mainland and buttressing it with a terrace set among the dizzy crags.

You might imagine that these solitary worshippers would be safe as they rose to pray with the dawn on their lonely island, but the world pursues you no matter to what remote fastness you fly. The Vikings found the little settlement and pillaged it four times in 812, 823, 833 and 839; although when you stand in these tiny dry-stone cells, with their austere stone cupboards, you wonder what wealth the poor monks could have possibly accumulated that was worth pillaging. Perhaps a silver cross or two dedicated to their founder, St Finian. Yet, they returned after each disaster and clung to their stern rock with moving devotion until at last, in the twelfth or thirteenth century, they were ordered to move and transferred themselves to the mainland monastery at Ballinskelligs. The salt wind now sighs in sympathy through the lichen-covered stone crosses and the long abandoned church.

Today the boats take the modern pilgrims out from such places as Knightstown; the

The stone pathway that wends its precarious way along the cliff edge

trip is a memorable one, although a landing cannot always be guaranteed when a heavy Atlantic swell is running. In early summer the Little Skellig is alive with breeding seabirds and now has an ever growing gannet colony. As the boat approaches the landing place on St Michael's islet the great white soaring birds shut their wings and plummet directly on to the fish like miniature divebombers. The puffins and the Manx shearwaters that swarm on the waters were all prized sources of food up to the end of the nineteenth century. No doubt they were also the mainstay of the monks' larder. It is to the monks that all thoughts eventually return on every visit to the Skelligs; to the atmosphere of prayer and devotion that still lingers among those simple beehive huts perched on the crags.

ABOVE: *The pathway up to the monastery*
ABOVE LEFT: *The Celtic cross that stands in the ruined monastery*
LEFT: *Looking across to Little Skellig*

*The remains of the
beehive cells in which the
monks lived until they left
for the mainland in the
twelfth or thirteenth
century. Little Skellig
can be seen in the distance*

S HERKIN MONASTERY, COUNTY CORK.
Sherkin Island lies about a mile offshore
near the little town of Baltimore; the outline
of the ruined monastery can be seen clearly
from the mainland among the hummocky
surfaces of the island. Thomas Davis' poem
starts with a vivid evocation of the geography of Sherkin.

> Old Inisherkin's crumbled face,
> looks like a moulting bird
> And in the calm and sleepy swell
> the ocean tide was heard.

The monastery was founded about 1460
by Dermot O'Driscoll, the paramount lord
of this corner of south-west Kerry, for the
Franciscan Friars of Strict Observance; the
fifteenth century was the great age of Franciscan building in Ireland. After the politic
submission of the great Irish nobles to
Richard II, the island did very much as it
liked, with the effective English power
confined to the Pale around Dublin. The
Franciscans had a strong appeal for
Irish-speaking Ireland and their Gothic-style
friaries multiplied exceedingly.

The Sherkin friary had enjoyed seventy or
eighty years of peaceful and prayerful exist-
ence when it was sacked and burnt – not this
time by the English or by Cromwell who
are the usual villains of the piece – but by the
Irish themselves. The men of Waterford
raided the island in an act of vengeance
against the O'Driscolls. The tower and sac-
risty seem to have been rebuilt after the raid,
but the abbey's prosperity was gone. The
O'Driscolls' power waned after they had
participated in the ill-fated Geraldine rebel-
lion and the ruined abbey passed into
English hands.

The monks returned for a short spell in 1627. The abbey, however, was in no condition to accommodate them and they had to build a house nearby. In the late seventeenth century the buildings suffered their final indignity when they were used as a pilchard curing shed. Today, the English owners, the monks and even the pilchards have long departed. The graceful ruins are quiet once more.

ABOVE, LEFT: *The interior of Sherkin monastery*
ABOVE, RIGHT: *Horseshoe Bay from Sherkin Island*

KNOWLTON CHURCH, DORSET. A strange site which sets the visitor a puzzle. The church, now a ruin, is of Norman construction with the characteristic rounded arches and square-set tower. It stands, however, in the central circle of a series of three prehistoric circles, lined up in a row near the main road between Cranborne and Wimborne. The circles mark henge-type monuments; nearby is a huge round barrow and several smaller barrows. The exact dates of all these constructions are not accurately known but there can be no question that they are many thousands of years older than the church.

Now the question arises – was the church deliberately placed in the centre of the largest circle in order to eliminate any traces of the old pagan worship? This would be done, of course, during the conversion of the local inhabitants to Christianity around the sixth and seventh centuries. The Norman church would have been erected later on the site of this first church. But who were the people who were converted – the Anglo-Saxon newcomers or the Celtic tribesmen, who had themselves displaced the earlier inhabitants of the area and who may have been the original creators of the henge-monuments? How much of their ancient ritual survived demanding to be exorcised by the building of a church? Mysteries we shall never solve!

GALLARUS ORATORY, COUNTY KERRY. Gallarus Oratory is the classic example of the boat-shaped oratories characteristic of County Kerry. It has a flat-headed doorway, with projecting stones inside, from which a curtain or even a door might have been hung. In the dim light from the one small window you see the walls curving up to meet, forming a roof overhead, and you get the strange feeling of worshipping God in an upturned boat.

Gallarus was an oratory with no monastery attached, although there is a cross-inscribed stone nearby. It may have been built much later, but the strong simplicity of its construction, like the beehive huts of Skellig Michael, takes you back in spirit to the early days of Christianity in Ireland; back to the Age of the Saints.

The faith came to Ireland from Wales; St Patrick was a romanized British Celt and in the generation that followed his labours Welsh monasticism inspired the beginnings of the movement in Ireland. But Irish monasticism soon gained a powerful impetus of its own. Although the early history of the Irish Church is still somewhat obscure and wrapped in controversy, by the sixth century the monk had become the leading figure in Irish Christianity. Saints like Columcille (St Columba), Aidan or Colman set out at this time to carry Christianity to distant heathen lands. Ireland had been the first country outside the boundaries of the old Roman Empire to be converted to the new faith, so it was natural for Irish missionaries to think of passing on the precious gift to countries that had, like Ireland, not undergone the discipline of Rome. St Columba converted Scotland and St Colman took the message to Burgundy.

At home, the monasteries began their illustrious career, which later made them memorable centres of art, learning and literature. They may not have had the architectural splendours of the great Gothic abbeys of the future, but in their beehive huts encircled by a high drystone wall, the monks produced such glories as the illuminated manuscript of the *Book of Kells*, and that masterpiece of metal work, the Ardagh Chalice. Even as they worked at their manuscripts they found time to jot down delightful lyrics in the margin. One old monk praised his little hermitage: 'A little lowly hidden hut besides cascades of the river, the swan's song, apple trees of great bounty . . . Will you come with me to see it.' As you stand in the Oratory at Gallarus you accept that warm invitation across the gap of a thousand years.

ABOVE LEFT: *The ruined Norman church at Knowlton within the prehistoric circular ditch*
LEFT: *The boat-shaped oratory*

THE MADONNA OF VALENCIA ISLAND, COUNTY KERRY. Throughout the centuries religiously-minded men have sought for shrines – places where the faithful can feel the inspiring presence of a Holy Spirit. At Mecca the Prophet Mohammed annexed the old pagan stone of the Kaaba as the central shrine of a new faith. At Knowlton, in Dorset, the newly-established Christian church was firmly planted in the middle of an old pagan ring, as if to annexe the area for the new religion. On Valencia Island on the south-west coast of Ireland a Roman Catholic priest, in our own time, has felt this same need to turn an old area of wreck and ruin into a new and exciting place of pilgrimage. He created a shrine in an old slate quarry.

The Silurian rocks of the west of Kerry lie on the rim of the Macgillycuddy's Reeks, the highest mountain range in Ireland. In remote geological times they were subject to much the same pressures as the similar beds in Snowdonia in Wales. This pressure also produced slate of excellent quality. In the mid-nineteenth century, a slate quarry was opened on the island; it eventually employed two hundred men. Not a large number when you compare it with the thousands employed in the quarries of North Wales. The slate was exported to England to furnish slabs for billiard tables, garden seats, butchers' tables and shelves for dairies. Eventually Valencia's distance from the centre of the market killed the trade. The quarry closed leaving the usual debris behind.

In the 1950s a Roman Catholic priest with vision came to the island. He saw the excavations and felt that he ought, as it were, to annexe them to a good cause. He placed statues of the Madonna among the torn rocks and a white rail, which calls to mind the one at Lourdes, in front of the grotto.

The bridge across to the mainland has made Valencia more accessible and it has become a popular resort for deep-sea fishing, aqua-lung diving and water-skiing. Perhaps the good priest built his grotto in the pious hope that a few visitors might spare a moment to visit it – and to think of higher things!

I ONA ISLAND, STRATHCLYDE. Everyone who writes about Iona seems to write in superlatives. Moray Maclaren wryly observed that this little island off the greater island of Mull has inspired some of the greatest Scottish painting and some of the feeblest. 'We have a certain amount of good writing about Iona,' he lamented 'and far more that is merely well-intentioned sentimentality touched with Celtic twilight sleep.' When you learn that the tourist steamers call regularly at Iona, that the ruined abbey has been restored, and that the island possesses a hotel and a golf course, you land with apprehension. You have come on a sort of pilgrimage. Here St Columba landed from Ireland in AD 563 in the hope of winning Scotland for Christianity. From Iona he set off on his perilous journeys through the Highlands and Islands. On the island he built his simple monastery which was later replaced by the present Abbey. Will you still find the old spirit of Iona amongst the tourists and in the restored church? Surprisingly, you do. Iona still casts its spell; the restored Abbey has an austere beauty. The gravestones of the early Scottish kings, from Kenneth MacAlpine to Macbeth, lie in the cloister garth, and the ruins of the conventual buildings are close at hand.

You walk amongst them and repeat the experience of Boswell and Dr Johnson who

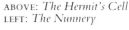
ABOVE: *The Hermit's Cell*
LEFT: *The Nunnery*

came here nearly two hundred years ago. Boswell, as he engagingly confesses, had come to Iona prepared to be disappointed. He walked among the ruins and, moved by the spirit of the place, dutifully resolved, for the hundredth time, to reform his course of life. 'I hoped that, ever after having been in this holy place, I should maintain an exemplary conduct.' Poor Boswell; his Iona mood didn't last long! Dr Johnson summed it all up in words of memorable rotundity that you can imagine fairly echoing across the grave of Macbeth, to the stunned bewilderment of the poor Highlanders.

We are now treading that illustrious Island, which was once the luminary of the Caledonian regions, whence savage clans and roving barbarians derived the benefits of knowledge, and the blessings of religion. To abstract the mind from all local emotion would be impossible if it were endeavoured and would be foolish if it were possible . . . Far from me and from my friends, be such frigid philosophy as may conduct us indifferent and unmoved over any ground which has been dignified by wisdom, bravery or virtue. That man is little to be envied whose patriotism would not gain force upon the field of Marathon, or whose piety would not grow warmer among the ruins of Iona!

After that, all one can add is a resounding 'Amen'.

ABOVE: *The ruined churches at Onaght*

RIGHT: *Corcomroe Abbey*

THE SEVEN CHURCHES, ARAN ISLANDS. This romantic collection of ecclesiastical ruins, parts of which date back to the eighth century, stands at Onaght at the western end of Inishmore, the largest island in the Aran group. The site is a fertile one for the rather windswept limestone landscape of these islands. The valley is sheltered with a stream running through it and wild garlic grows boldly among the broken walls. The title of the site is, however, a misnomer: the complex consists of two churches and their attached buildings. No doubt the monks were attracted to the site by the relatively rich soil of the area. St Brecan was the founder of the first church on the island and near it is the base of a decorated cross shaft which marks the grave of the Saint himself. Why should we doubt it? The grave was opened in 1822 in the presence of the distinguished Irish scholar, Dr Petrie, and a slab was found with the Saint's name inscribed on it. Many cures are claimed for this venerated spot. Nearby is a group of memorial stones; one bears a Latin dedication, the interpretation of which is, very properly, wrapped in mystery.

CORCOMROE ABBEY, COUNTY CLARE. This twelfth-century abbey had the delightful and well deserved name of Sancta Maria de Petra Fertile, 'Saint Mary of the Fertile Rock'. The ruins lie in a valley which is rich in green grass in the spring – a rarity in the barren limestone district of the Burren, in County Clare. It was a Cistercian foundation, inspired by the great change that came over Irish monasticism after 1142. Ireland's leading churchman of the period, St Malachy of Armagh, had visited St Bernard at Clairvaux and had been deeply impressed by the austere purity of the Cistercian rule. The monks lived under a strict discipline; it was the end of the pleasantly lax, friendly, human type of Irish monasticism which had flourished from the early days of St Patrick. No more beehive huts grouped around a small chapel and surrounded by a drystone wall! Corcomroe's architecture is far more ambitious. The site is rich in Romanesque carving; the stern Cistercians had not yet got the exuberant, imaginative Irish stonemasons under control. Alas, no matter, which rule prevailed, all came to ruin in the end.

The remains of
the nave of
Corcomroe
Abbey

INISHCALTRA, COUNTY CLARE. These ruins, which stand on an island in Loch Dearg, form a collection of churches, tombs, round towers and anchorite cells which cover a long period of Irish history. Here again, is one of those Irish places of pilgrimage which gains immensely by the way you approach it. You can race to it by motor boat but it is better to row out in your hired boat. This was surely the way St Caimin travelled when he came to found the first monastery on the island in the seventh century.

It did not, however, remain permanently in peace; the Vikings burnt the church in 836 and harried it again in 933. Brian Boru, High King of Ireland, is said to have built one of the churches on the island. This is possible, for his brother was abbot here and he would surely have persuaded the great High King to support the community.

ABOVE: *The altar in Caimine Church*
RIGHT ABOVE: *The view from the west of the island in Inishcaltra*
RIGHT BELOW: *The altar in Teampull Mhuire Church.*

The most prominent of the ruins – apart from the round tower, are of slightly later date and include the thirteenth-century church of St Mary. All the architectural glory had vanished by the seventeenth century. Maybe it is the isolation of its island site that gives this holy place its particularly attractive atmosphere. You sympathize with the grief of the Guest Master Ammchad who was ordered to leave around 1043 because he had, with true Irish hospitality, offered a guest wine. No wonder he shut himself up for ten years in a cell in Germany!

189

The remains of the monastery buildings stand amid the peace of Inishcaltra Island

BURIAL GROUNDS

To muse and brood and live again in memory,
With those old faces of our infancy
Heaped over with a mound of grass
Two handfuls of white dust, shut in an urn
of brass!
ALFRED, LORD TENNYSON

CAULDSIDE BURN, DUMFRIES & GALLOWAY

PUICIN AN COUR, COUNTY KERRY

DUNCRAIGAIG CAIRN, LOCHGILPHEAD,
STRATHCLYDE

PENTRE IFAN CROMLECH, DYFED

BEINN-NA-CAILLICH, SKYE

Duncraigaig Cairn, Strathclyde

CAULDSIDE BURN, DUMFRIES & GALLOWAY. At the head of Cauldside Burn on the lowest slopes of Cairnbarrow Hill and within a few miles of the waters of Wigtown Bay in south-west Scotland is this small but fascinating collection of many of the elements we have included in our secret landscapes – from cairns to cup and ring marks, from standing stones to small stone circles. Here, too, is the final element that completes our evocation in pictures of the spirit of our distant past. In the largest mound is a cist, a box-like structure built of heavy stones. It marks a burial site of later date than the great long barrows, but still carries us back to the distant past, reminding us of the fears and hopes of our ancient forebears when confronted with the basic, inescapable fact of death.

On a misty day the television mast on the nearby hill rises like a ghostly guardian over the heavy stones of the cairn, stones that preceded it by at least 4000 years. In our modern television age are our emotions and feelings so very different from those of our ancestors when a loved or great person passes away? We, too, want to see him nobly commemorated. We will never know who was laid to rest in the stone cist at Cauldside Burn, but we can imagine the long procession climbing the hill, the chanting, the lamentation and the sense of loss among the tribesmen as the High Chief was placed in his grave. Did the idea for these burial cairns and the earlier and more elaborate passage graves filter across Europe from the more advanced civilizations of the Middle East? Are they barbaric versions of the gloriously rich, treasure-filled tomb of Tutankhamun in distant Egypt? It is more likely that they were created locally and independently to meet the needs of the people of Western Europe.

The wind blows among the old cists, dolmens and cromlechs of Britain and we feel, as A. E. Housman felt as he looked at the Roman ruins of Viroconium (Wroxeter).

The tree of man was never quiet:
Then 'twas the Roman; now 'tis I.

PUICIN AN COUR, COUNTY KERRY. This burial place lies high on a hillside in the Dingle peninsula on the west coast of Ireland. The mountains plunge steeply to the sea all around and the air seems always full of salt from the Atlantic spray. The grave itself is an interesting variation on the usual theme of the megalithic tombs of Ireland. The most impressive of these structures are the passage graves which come to their grand climax at New Grange in the Boyne valley. There the passage leads deep into a great mound ending in a chamber with a magnificent corbelled roof. The glory of New Grange, however, lies in the decoration of some of the stones; spirals and fern-shaped carvings twist and twine on the hard stone surface in a way that suggests, across the mists of 2000 years, the sinuous, richly-coloured illuminations of the *Book of Kells*.

Perhaps the Celts, and the mysterious races who preceded them and who built not only New Grange but the humbler Puicin an Cour on its rain-soaked hillside in the far west, may have felt that strange persuasive charm of Ireland which entices men to think not in stern straight lines but in entrancing curves.

Puicin an Cour may be somewhat later in date than New Grange. Carbon-14 tests suggest that structures of this type were built in Ireland about 2000 BC, maybe by a new wave of invaders. These newcomers modified the shape of the long mounds of the passage graves into a wedge; and made a straighter forecourt in front of it for whatever ceremonies they performed for their honoured dead.

DUNCRAIGAIG CAIRN, LOCHGILPHEAD, STRATHCLYDE. This cairn lies in a little wood near the road and has probably been pillaged in the past. It was originally 100 ft in diameter and is still 7 ft high. Cremated bones and other burials have been found in it. Cists were also discovered in the mound, which contained fragments of pottery and a food vessel. This ruined heap of stones must have been of great importance to the Bronze Age inhabitants who lived in this area around 1500 BC. When they piled the stones up into Duncraigaig Cairn they must have hoped that they were raising a memorial that would stand as unchanging as the Argyll hills around it. But through the long centuries the landscape of Britain has been constantly changing; even the hills and the coastline change slowly and surely and the soil and vegetation they nurture change too.

The first Mesolithic hunters who entered this part of Scotland found a bare tundra region, left behind by the retreat of the ice. Game, however, would have been plentiful and the rivers swarmed with fish. As the climate grew warmer, the forest advanced to conquer the tundra, and Man had to adapt to the new conditions. Each incoming wave of settlers had to battle against the forest or clear the open land of stones; the builders of the cairn at Duncraigaig must have known exactly what labour is involved in this.

The great Caledonian Forest laid its dense blanket of trees over the landscape of Scotland well into historic times. The kings of Scotland sometimes burnt great sections of it to scare out the game for hunting. The trees that now stand guard around Duncraigaig are mere striplings – arboreal newcomers.

PENTRE IFAN CROMLECH, DYFED. It is arguable that this is the finest cromlech that Wales – that nursery of cromlechs – has to show. It stands, as so many prehistoric structures seem to do, in a landscape of sweeping views over land and sea on the western slopes of the magical Presely Hills in Dyfed (North Pembrokeshire). Behind it are the strange rock outcrops called Cerrig Merbion Owen – the Rocks of Owen's Sons. The ancient stones of Pentre Ifan had been standing in their lonely place thousands of years before the mediaeval sons of Owen, whoever he was, haunted these hillsides. The great capstone seems to be precariously balanced almost on the points of the four thin supporting rocks.

The cromlech itself represents the actual burial chamber, which, in its original state, was buried deep under a covering mound of earth and stone. This seems to have been removed in the comparatively distant past, maybe by early treasure seekers. Could these have been the wild Sons of Owen? These great burial mounds went on attracting amateur explorers until the early nineteenth century. Many an archaeologically-minded country squire of the Regency period would invite his neighbours to join him in 'cracking a cromlech' on his estate, to be followed by an elaborate picnic on the spot – 'grouse pie washed down by champagne' were promised on one letter of invitation. Infuriating reading for the modern, highly-trained professional archaeologists who have found nearly all these great megalithic grave structures already pillaged.

The outline of the Pentre Ifan grave mound has recently been marked out around the central stones of the burial chamber. The visitor can now see that these huge long barrows were not simply burial places. Two mounds project like horns from the portal of the cromlech and could delimit a sort of forecourt in which ceremonies could be performed. Were the noble dead worshipped here or rites performed, as in Egypt, to ensure them a safe passage to another world? We cannot know for certain.

B EINN-NA-CAILLICH, SKYE. Our last glimpse of a secret landscape – a lonely burial chamber on a bare hill top in the island of Skye. The high mountains stand guard over it. The old hymn declared:

> Before the hills in order stood
> Or Earth received her frame . . .

but, in truth, our earth in Britain received its frame from the hard work of men over thousands of years – men whose leaders in the second millennium BC might have been buried in graves like Beinn-na-Caillich. The archaeologists, with their modern dating techniques and their exciting new theories that range from the significance of the Elm Decline in the third millennium to the Central Place Theory, which discusses

the siting of the large hill forts on the chalk-lands of the South, are gradually building up a picture of how our remote forebears mastered the harsh environment they found when they first arrived in Britain. They show us the forest being cleared through the long centuries. Then men set up their graves, their stone circles, their forts – and later their castles, churches and fields.

Under the pattern of present-day agriculture lies a far older pattern left by the pioneers. Sometimes it shows through, like the writing on a mediaeval palimpsest, and makes us realize that it is through its secret landscapes that England, and all Britain, became Blake's 'green and pleasant land'.

GRID REFERENCES

England, Wales and Scotland: Ordnance Survey 1:50,000 series   Eire: Ordnance Survey 1:126720 series

1 LIVING PLACES

1 Dun Carloway, Isle of Lewis, Outer Hebrides
Grid ref: Sheet 13 192414

2 Clochán na Carraige, Inishmore, Aran Islands
Grid ref: Sheet 14 815105

3 A Cheviot Hill Enclosure, Northumberland
Grid ref: Sheet 81 152005

4 Lulworth, Dorset
Grid ref: Sheet 194 882803

5 The Lone Shieling, Eigg, Inner Hebrides
Grid ref: Sheet 39 455842

6 Din Lligwy, Anglesey, Gwynedd
Grid ref: Sheet 114 496863

7 Hallsands, Devon
Grid ref: Sheet 202 818384

8 The Ruined Black House (Strath na Creitheach), Skye
Grid ref: Sheet 32 228507

9 Glen Gloy, Isle of Arran
Grid ref: Sheet 69 347998

10 Dun nan Gall Broch, Isle of Mull
Grid ref: Sheet 48 433435

11 Bray Tower, Valencia Island
Grid ref: Sheet 20 303702

2 FORTIFICATIONS

12 Dun Aengus, Inishmore, Aran Islands
Grid ref: Sheet 14 815098

13 An Sgurr Hill Fort, Eigg, Inner Hebrides
Grid ref: Sheet 39 462847

14 Chew Green Roman Camp, Northumberland
Grid ref: Sheet 80 085787

15 Cahercommaun Stone Fort, County Clare
Grid ref: Sheet 14 017310

16 Dunadd, Strathclyde
Grid ref: Sheet 55 937838

17 Tre'r Ceiri, Gwynedd
Grid ref: Sheet 123 374447

18 Dun Onaght, Inishmore, Aran Islands
Grid ref: Sheet 14 810102

19 Trusty's Hill Fort, Dumfries & Galloway
Grid ref: Sheet 83 560587

20 Carrock Fell Hill Fort, Cumbria
Grid ref: Sheet 90 338343

21 Staigue Fort, County Kerry
Grid ref: Sheet 24 633608

22 Great Bernera, Isle of Lewis, Outer Hebrides
Grid ref: Sheet 13 357156

23 Dun Mhuirich, Strathclyde
Grid ref: Sheet 55 844723

24 The Lost Dun (Dun Loch Michean), Strathclyde
Grid ref: Sheet 55 987802

25 Hadrian's Wall, Northumberland
Grid ref: Sheet 86 666681

26 Carrigafoyle Castle, County Kerry
Grid ref: Sheet 17 990475

27 Minard Castle, County Kerry
Grid ref: Sheet 20 985540

28 Carnasserie Castle, Strathclyde
Grid ref: Sheet 55 008838

29 Dunamore Castle, Cape Clear Island, County Cork
Grid ref: Sheet 24 956222

30 O'Brien's Castle, Inisheer, Aran Islands
Grid ref: Sheet 14 987012

31 Leamaneh Castle, County Clare
Grid ref: Sheet 14 935235

32 Girnigoe and Sinclair Castles, Wick
Grid ref: Sheet 12 388549

33 Castlekirke, County Galway
Grid ref: Sheet 11 996502

34 Clifden Castle, County Galway
Grid ref: Sheet 10 638517

35 Rahinnane Castle, County Kerry
Grid ref: Sheet 20 025368

36 Kilcoe Castle, County Cork
Grid ref: Sheet 24 018343

3 WORKING PLACES

37 The Killhope Wheel, County Durham
Grid ref: Sheet 87 827431

38 Greenburn Beck Lead Mine, Cumbria
Grid ref: Sheet 90 023290

39 Old Coke Ovens, County Durham
Grid ref: Sheet 92 116398

40 Abereiddi Bay, Dyfed
Grid ref: Sheet 157 795315

41 The Lost Carriage, Near Chesters, Northumberland
Grid ref: Sheet 87 919706

42 Old Gang Smelt Mill, Swaledale, Yorkshire
Grid ref: Sheet 91 965009

43 The Deserted Jetty, Inisheer, Aran Islands
Grid ref: Sheet 14 992011

44 Charcoal Burning Site, Newby Bridge, Lake District
Grid ref: Sheet 96 878346

45 Parys Mountain, Anglesey, Gwynedd
Grid ref: Sheet 114 444906

46 The Stranded Coaster, Inisheer, Aran Islands
Grid ref: Sheet 14 995015

47 Powder Mills, Dartmoor, Devon
Grid ref: Sheet 191 773628

4 PLACES OF PAGAN WORSHIP

48 Kintraw Standing Stone, Strathclyde
Grid ref: Sheet 55 050830

49 Castlerigg Stone Circle, Cumbria
Grid ref: Sheet 90 236294

50 The Ring of Brodgar, Orkney Islands
Grid ref: Sheet 6 294133

51 Stenness Henge and Standing Stones, Orkney Islands
Grid ref: Sheet 6 125307

52 Callanish Standing Stones, Isle of Lewis, Outer Hebrides
Grid ref: Sheet 13 331214

53 Achnabreck Cup-and-ring Markings, Strathclyde
Grid ref: Sheet 55 907856

54 Carn Meini, Dyfed
Grid ref: Sheet 145 144324

5 THE COMING OF CHRISTIANITY

55 Skellig Michael, County Kerry
Grid ref: Sheet 20 610259

56 Sherkin Monastery, County Cork
Grid ref: Sheet 24 030225

57 Knowlton Church, Dorset
Grid ref: Sheet 195 024103

58 Gallarus Oratory, County Kerry
Grid ref: Sheet 20 395052

59 The Madonna of Valencia Island, County Kerry
Grid ref: Sheet 20 385775

60 Iona Island, Strathclyde
Grid ref: Sheet 48 277248 (Hermit's Cell)
Sheet 48 284241 (Nunnery)

61 The Seven Churches, Inishmore, Aran Islands
Grid ref: Sheet 14 812120

62 Corcomroe Abbey, County Clare
Grid ref: Sheet 14 089297

63 Inishcaltra, County Clare
Grid ref: Sheet 15 850698

6 BURIAL GROUNDS

64 Cauldside Burn, Dumfries & Galloway
Grid ref: Sheet 83 573529

65 Puicin an Cour, County Kerry
Grid ref: Sheet 20 985509

66 Duncraigaig Cairn, Lochgilphead, Strathclyde
Grid ref: Sheet 55 966834

67 Pentre Ifan Cromlech, Dyfed
Grid ref: Sheet 145 099370

68 Beinn-na-Caillich, Skye
Grid ref: Sheet 32 221627

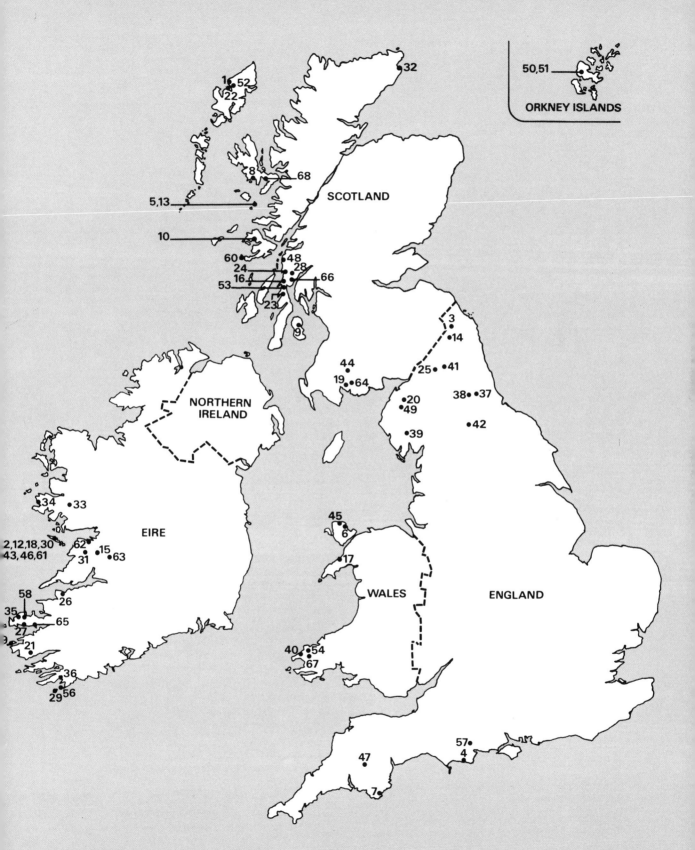

1 52
22

32

50,51
ORKNEY ISLANDS

8
68

5,13

10

SCOTLAND

60
48
24
28
16
66
53
23

9

3
14

44
25 41
19 64

38 37
20
49

42

39

NORTHERN
IRELAND

34 33

EIRE

45
6

2,12,18,30
62
43,46,61
31
15
63

17

58
26
WALES
ENGLAND

35
65
27

21

40 54
67

36
29 56

57
4

47

7

GLOSSARY

Barrow
A stone or earth mound built above a burial. Barrows were used from Neolithic until Saxon times. *See also* Bell Barrow, Disc Barrow, Long Barrow, Saucer Barrow, Tump, Tumulus.

Beaker Folk
People that came to Britain in about 2000 BC. They are named from their practice of placing pottery beakers (drinking cups) in the barrows alongside their dead.

Bell Barrow
A round, Early Bronze Age burial mound separated from its surrounding ditch by a level area of ground (berm). Bell barrows usually cover male burials and are found in the south of England. *See also* Berm.

Berm
The level area of ground that lies between the mound and ditch of bell and disc barrows.

Broch
A circular fortified tower, the rooms of which are built within its dry stone walls. Brochs are found in northern Scotland and in the Orkney and Shetland Islands.

Bronze Age
The period between about 2000 BC and 600 BC, during which Man made many of his tools and weapons from bronze.

Cairn
A construction built largely or entirely of stones, invariably the remnants of the covering of a burial, from which the surrounding earth of the barrow has been carried or weathered away.

Celts
A cultural and linguistic group who until 900 BC lived in central Europe, and then spread across western Europe and the eastern Mediterranean.

Chert
A hard sedimentary rock that is easily chipped to form a sharp cutting edge. It was used throughout the Stone Age to make tools and weapons.

Cist
A small, stone-lined burial chamber.

Coloniae
Towns built by the Romans for the specific purpose of housing retired soldiers who would, if necessary, provide a reserve line of defence in the event of a native uprising.

Crannog
An ancient lake dwelling built on a platform of logs and brushwood. Found in Ireland and Scotland.

Cromlech
A megalithic tomb consisting of a large, flat stone resting horizontally on three or more vertical stones from which the soil that once covered it has been removed. Found in England, especially in Devon and Cornwall, Wales and Ireland. In Brittany such a structure is referred to as a dolmen (table-stone) and the word 'cromlech' refers to a circle of standing stones.

Cup-and-ring Markings
Small circular depressions cut into rock and sometimes surrounded by carved rings. They are usually found in northern England and Scotland on standing stones and on the walls of burial chambers.

Disc Barrow
Constructed during the Early Bronze Age, often covering female burials, it consists of a small mound in the centre of a large circular platform, surrounded by a ditch and an outer bank.

Dolmen
The remains of a ruined burial chamber. In France the structure referred to in Britain as a cromlech (*qv*) is called a dolmen.

Druids
Members of a Celtic priesthood living in Gaul and Britain from about the first century BC. They led local resistance against the Romans and were finally crushed in Anglesey in AD 61 by Paulinus.

Dun
A Scottish Iron Age fort which, unlike the larger broch (*qv*), does not have circular walls.

Henge Monument
An area of ground used for religious rites in the Neolithic and Bronze Ages. It often contained a wooden or stone circle, and was bounded by a ditch and a bank. The types are classified by the number of entrances they had.

Inhumation
The burial of a corpse (i.e. not cremation).

Iron Age
The period between the end of the Bronze Age (about 600 BC) and the Roman period (but which extended through the early centuries AD and beyond the Roman departure in areas outside Roman rule (e.g. in Ireland and Scotland).

Long Barrow
An elongated, oval-shaped barrow usually dating from the Neolithic period.

Megalithic
A term describing a monument such as a large single stone, a circle of large stones or a burial chamber.

Mesolithic
The middle period of the Stone Age (c. 10,000–4000 BC), essentially that of a hunter-gatherer economy.

Midden
A prehistoric refuse pit.

Mile-castle
A Roman watch tower; one of a series built along Hadrian's Wall at intervals of about one mile in between the major forts.

Monolith
A single large standing stone erected for ritual or ceremonial purposes.

Neolithic
The New Stone Age (c. 4000–2000 BC). A period during which communities began to settle, cultivate crops and use pottery. Stone tools and weapons were made to a high standard, especially in their polish and finish.

Ogam (Ogham)
An alphabet used in Britain and Ireland around the fifth century AD. It consisted of twenty characters, each formed by making vertical and diagonal strokes on or across a straight line.

Palaeolithic
The Old Stone Age (c. 500,000–10,000 BC). During this period man began to make simple stone tools.

Passage Grave
A burial chamber covered by a cairn and approached by a straight passage.

Pele-tower
A small, square, fortified tower dating from the Middle Ages. Usually found along the English-Scottish border.

Perisalith
A line of stones surrounding a long or round barrow.

Radiocarbon Dating
A method of dating archaeological organic material up to 70,000 years old by measuring its content of radio-active carbon–14, which decays with a half-life of $5,730 \pm 40$ years.

Revetment
A support of stone, timber or turf built around a rampart or burial ground to prevent the sides from slipping or collapsing.

Round Barrow
A circular burial mound, with or without a surrounding ditch, used from the Early Bronze Age until Saxon times.

Sarsens
Large blocks of sandstone often used in the building of stone monuments, especially the trilithons at Stonehenge.

Saucer Barrow
A Bronze Age low circular mound surrounded by a ditch and usually covering a female cremation burial.

Standing Stones
Large stones placed in an upright position for some religious, astronomical or architectural purpose.

Stone Age
The period during which metals were unknown to Man and tools and weapons were made from stone. The Stone Age is divided into three periods: Palaeolithic, Mesolithic and Neolithic.

Storage Pits
Pits, generally dug into chalk and varying in size but usually about 3 ft wide and 6 ft deep, in which food, especially grain was stored. They are found on Late Bronze Age and Iron Age settlement sites.

Timber-lacing
A method of reinforcing a hill-top rampart by placing horizontal timbers through the rampart and connecting them to vertical posts at the front and rear.

Trilithon
Three stones, two of which are set upright and the third laid horizontally across their tops (as at Stonehenge).

Tump
A barrow or burial mound, but used to refer to the small mound at the centre of a disc barrow.

Tumulus
A barrow.

Vitrified Fort
A fort, the stone walls of which have been subjected to such intense heat that they have fused into an almost glassy mass. The extreme heat was produced when the timber-lacing (qv) through the walls was burnt, generally because of enemy action.

FURTHER READING

The essential equipment for the beginner setting out to explore the archaeological wealth of Britain must be a small library of guide books. Luckily there has been a whole series of such books produced in recent years, written by experts and covering every section of the country. The Department of the Environment has produced six guides to the ancient monuments and historic buildings under its care which are detailed on the Government Publications Sectional List, no 27. Other experts have covered special sections of England. Recommended guides for particular areas include:

James Dyer. *Southern England: An Archaeological Guide* (Faber, 1973)
Aileen Fox. *South-West England, 3500BC –600AD* (2nd Ed. David & Charles, 1973)
Ronald Jessup. *South-East England* (Thames & Hudson, 1970)
R. Rainbird Clarke. *East Anglia* (EP Publishing Ltd, 1971)

Scotland has been well covered by Richard Feachem in his *Guide to Prehistoric Scotland* (B. T. Batsford, 1977) and by Euan Mackie in *Scotland: An Archaeological Guide* (Faber, 1975). For Wales, we have the help of Christopher Houlder's *Wales, an Archaeological Guide* (Faber, 1975). The Republic of Ireland is covered by Peter Harbison in his *Guide to the National Monuments of Ireland* (Gill and Macmillan, 1970). More general guides are Jacquetta Hawkes' well known *Guide to the Prehistoric and Roman Monuments in England and Wales* of which a new edition was published in 1973 (Phillips Park Press). Peter Clayton includes the whole of Britain in his *Archaeological Sites in Britain* (Weidenfeld & Nicolson, 1976).

Many of these authors, such as Jacquetta Hawkes, Peter Clayton, Peter Harbison in Ireland and Richard Feachem in Scotland, include valuable outlines of the developments in prehistory, and guide the beginner through the complexities of Mesolithic, Neolithic, Bronze Age and Iron Age chronology. Collins *Field Guide to Archaeology in Britain*, by Eric S. Wood (2nd Ed. 1974) also introduces you to the actual techniques of the modern archaeologist.

Once the 'archaeology bug' has firmly gripped you, you will find your own way to the wider more specialized literature of the subject, but three books can help you towards this wider study. Professor Glyn Daniel's fascinating *The Idea of Prehistory* (Peter Smith, 1974) traces the way the study of the remote past has developed in Western history. Aubrey Burl has produced the first comprehensive survey of all *The Stone Circles of the British Isles* (Yale University Press, 1979), and has included valuable summaries of all the recent theories on the subject. Richard Bradley, in the *Prehistoric Settlement of Britain* (Routledge & Kegan Paul Ltd, 1978), explores the way early man conquered his environment to create the landscape of Britain. This book is one of a projected series, edited by Professor Barry Cunliffe, which will summarize the most modern research on the archaeology of Britain. Professor Cunliffe himself has written: *Iron Age Communities in Britain* (Routledge & Kegan Paul Ltd, 1974). When the series is completed, it will be indispensable to every student of prehistory – experts as well as beginners.

PHOTOGRAPHER'S NOTE

While photographing the widely varied locations I selected for *Secret Landscapes*, grey and wet weather seemed to befriend me. 'Befriend' is the correct word because, in hindsight, it was good lighting for a lot of the locations; the wet weather provided a backdrop of mysterious grey.

When the sun did break free of the clouds and run over the hills, my camera would get dashed about in my excitement at the new shapes in the landscape. A small battle would ensue: to get the tripod vertical and camera horizontal, to fumble with the Weston and to adjust stops on the lens – all before the light went. To lose this battle is to lose the picture and only the photographer knows what he has missed.

Rough terrain and these battles with my equipment eventually broke both the cameras I was using. My MPP 5×4 bounced down the rock cliffs of Skellig Michael and landed with a flat thud on the pathway twenty-five feet below. Later on Iona, while scrambling around the Hermit's Cell, I fell, camera first, on to an old stone wall, smashing my Mamiya Press 6×9 cm.

I used Ilford FP4 film, both 5×4 and 120 sizes rated at 80 ASA. The 5×4 film, which was used only for the Irish locations, was developed in an ID11 deep tank and the 120 in Perceptol. No filters were used.

All the negatives were printed in my darkroom with a cold cathode enlarger on Agfa Record Rapid paper.

Michael Hales

Dun Carloway, Outer Hebrides

INDEX